YOU'VE GOT Retirement QUESTIONS?
WE'VE GOT ANSWERS

by Lynn Toomey, RetireMentor

© 2022 Lynn Toomey

All rights reserved. No portion of this book may be reproduced, stored in a retrieval system, or transmitted in any form or by any means – electronic, mechanical, photocopy, recording, scanning, or other, except for brief quotations in critical reviews or articles, without the prior written permission of the author.

As you read this book, please let us know if you find any errors as this is our first edition and we've can't possibly proof-read any longer. LOL.

Should you have any questions about the content of this book, or your retirement, please email us at: retire@herretirement.com. To learn more about Her Retirement, visit: www.HerRetirement.com
To schedule a chat with author Lynn Toomey, visit: www.GetHerDoneChat.com

About the Author Lynn Toomey

Lynn is a retirement educator, researcher, writer and founder of Her Retirement and Retirement Power Hours, as well as co-founder of Your Retirement Advisor. At 57, she's getting a bit more serious about her own retirement, but really has no plans to call it quits on what she loves doing…empowering people with education and financial wellness. She can be reached while enjoying and juggling her favorite "F" words: family, finances, full time work, friends, fitness, food, fashion, field trips, freedom and fun. at lynnt@herretirement.com.

For my mom

"My mother has taught me some valuable lessons throughout my life, but the most important was that I could be the "her" in hero. Independence and financial wellness was and is an important foundational element…along with health and happiness. I've taken this to heart every day of my life and I've created several financial education platforms to help women be the hero of their own stories."

The Big Book of Retirement Questions & Answers
by Her Retirement

78 million people are retiring over the next 10 years and they all want to know how to solve the challenges of retirement.

The Big Book of Retirement Questions & Answers contains a collection of 90 questions I've heard over the past five years from hosting retirement planning classes at colleges, universities, and online. I decided to research each one and determine what the retirement experts and academics in the retirement planning space have to say about these important questions. These are critical questions all pre-retirees and those just in retirement should be asking, and getting objective answers for.

I address 15 different areas of challenge, concern, and opportunity as you prepare for and transition into retirement. My mission is to empower you and everyone with the knowledge needed to make informed decisions about your finances and retirement. I do believe that by knowing more, you can quite possibly know more…now and in retirement. I also want you to create and implement a retirement plan you not only understand but have 100% confidence in. I hope this book helps.

This book isn't fancy. It is, however, factual and devoid of "fluff". The 107 pages of content are in an easy-to-read question-and-answer format, with the answer being based on "What the research says" vs. the biases of an investment advisor or insurance agent. As a retirement educator, I've done my homework to give you as much balanced and objective information on as many retirement topics as possible.

- Retirement Planning
- Retirement Risks
- Debt
- Income in Retirement
- Social Security
- Home Equity
- Savings & Investments in Retirement
- 401(k)/IRA Savings
- Taxes in Retirement
- Insurance
- Healthcare in Retirement
- Long-Term Care
- College Funding
- Estate Planning
- Getting Help

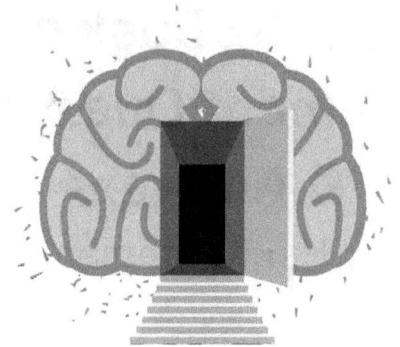

If you open your mind, you'll learn the following in this book:

- The importance of a written retirement plan and all the components that SHOULD be included
- Key strategies to make what have more efficient and sustainable without adding any additional money
- How to determine safe withdrawal rate regardless of market performance (and avoid the common mistake that drains retirement funds 15+ years early)
- The most effective way to protect yourself from market crashes & rising taxes in retirement and keep your retirement fund completely unphased, even it tax rates double
- How to pay as little taxes in retirement as possible, even zero
- How to minimize risk in your portfolio and protect against market downturns while positioning it to take advantage of potential market growth
- How to mitigate the major risks you may face in retirement
- What you can do now, pre-retirement, to help improve your outcome.
- How to protect against tax rate creep, that many experts believe is a given
- Why the "traditional" approach to retirement planning and the "traditional" advisor may not be the best approach
- How to protect yourself, your spouse and your family with healthcare, long term care and estate planning solutions and more

If you want to commit some time to improving your retirement outcome, want to avoid the potential blind spots and landmines you may face in retirement, and better prepare yourself for the retirement you've imagined, then this book is for you. Welcome.

"An investment in knowledge pays the best interest."

-Benjamin Franklin

Retirement Planning

Question 1: Do you understand the importance of a written retirement plan?
What the Research Says: *"Those who have a written retirement plan have a nest egg 445% bigger than non-planners."* –HSBC, Future of Retirement, 2013[1]

If this quote doesn't convince you, nothing will. But let's look at why pre-retirees today *must* have a written retirement plan.

- Reason 1: Because we're living longer. (See question 7 about longevity risk.)
- Reason 2: Because the funding burden is on us. Traditional pension plans are going away. People are responsible for building their own retirement savings in the form of 401ks, 403bs and IRAs. Retirement funding used to come from a combination of defined benefit pension and Social Security.[2] In 1998, 59% of Fortune 500 companies offered a defined benefit plan, or pension.[3] By 2018, that figure had dropped to 15%.[4]
- Reason 3: To squelch our fears. "61% of baby boomers fear running out of money more than they fear death."[5]
- Reason 4: To understand our income needs. "81% of us don't know how much money we need to retire."[6]
- Reason 5: To create a bigger nest egg. "84% of us don't have a written retirement plan."[7]
- Reason 6: To control our behaviors. Everyone has the temptation to chase returns and make uninformed, knee-jerk reactions as the volatile markets move up and down. In fact, these behaviors have been proven in numerous studies to negatively impact portfolios over the long term. The Dalbar study shown below illustrates that the average investor had returns of 2.5% while the S&P was at 9.2%.

---

[1] HSBC, *The Future of Retirement: A Balancing Act*, 2013, https://www.hsbc.ca/1/PA_ES_Content_Mgmt/content/canada4/pdfs/personal/for-balancing-act-global-report.pdf.
[2] Larry DeWitt, "The Development of Social Security in America," *Social Security Bulletin*, Vol. 70, No. 3, 2010, https://www.ssa.gov/policy/docs/ssb/v70n3/v70n3p1.html.
[3] Lee Barney, "A Mere 16% of Fortune 500 Companies Offer a DB Plan," *PLANADVISER*, March 2, 2018, https://www.planadviser.com/mere-16-fortune-500-companies-offer-db-plan/.
[4] DeWitt, "The Development of Social Security in America," *Social Security Bulletin*.
[5] Allianz Life Insurance Company, "Outliving Your Money Feared More Than Death," *News Release*, June 17, 2010, https://www.allianzlife.com/~/media/files/allianz/documents/reclaiming-the-future/rtf_6_17_2010.pdf.
[6] Merrill Lynch, "Finances in Retirement: New Challenges, New Solutions," *AgeWave*, 2017, https://agewave.com/what-we-do/landmark-research-and-consulting/research-studies/finances-in-retirement-new-challenges-new-solutions/.
[7] Transamerica Center for Retirement Studies, *17th Annual Transamerica Retirement Survey*, December 2016, https://www.transamericacenter.org/docs/default-source/retirement-survey-of-workers/tcrs2016_sr_retirement_survey_of_workers_compendium.pdf.

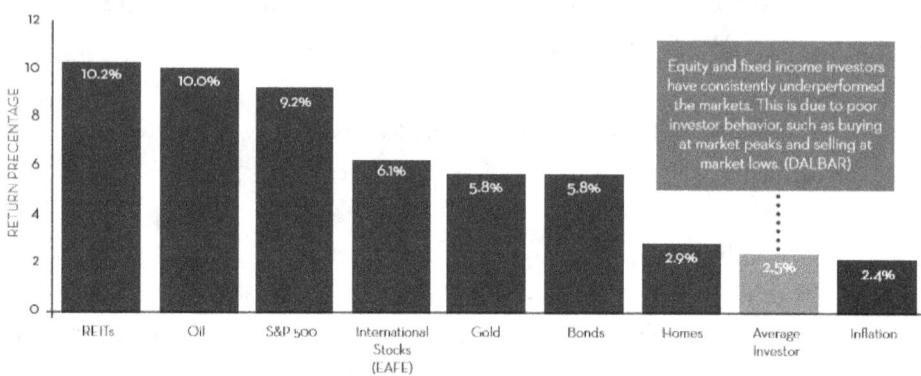

For these reasons and more, it's imperative to make a commitment to creating a retirement plan and putting it in writing.

Question 2: If you are a woman, do you understand the issues that are unique to women that a written retirement plan can help address?

What the Research Says: For many women, their reasons for proper (and written) retirement planning are even more significant. Unlike their male counterparts, women face some formidable challenges when it comes to finances and retirement. Women typically live longer and make less (women who work full-time earn, on average, about 82% of what men earn.[8] Women also save less, invest less, and take career breaks. And, though they are more likely to participate in an employer's savings plan, they have a retirement savings gap.

According to a Vanguard study, men have 50% higher balances in their retirement plans than women, even though women are 11% more likely to participate in a retirement plan than men. They have a great likelihood of living alone and they also face higher healthcare costs (not due to health, but to longevity). Women are typically primary decision-makers for purchases but are less confident in financial decisions.

The good news, however, is that women are planners and doers, researchers, and knowledge seekers. Women can be pragmatic when it comes to their finances, but there's an element of emotion that also influences their decision-making. They are more averse to risk, which can be a good thing in retirement. A BlackRock study of 4,000 investors found that women on average

---

[8] U.S. Bureau of Labor Statistics, "Women in the Labor Force: A Databook," *BLS Reports*, November 2017, https://www.bls.gov/opub/reports/womens-databook/2017/home.htm.

hold more conservative investments than male investors.[9] Women are more cautious…making data-backed decisions. They're also intuitive and determined. And they aren't afraid to ask for directions! It's worth noting that women are expected to be the recipients of the largest wealth transfer in history. Women: now is the time to understand your wealth. According to Investopedia's article, *Women and the Great Wealth Transfer* (June 2019),[10] the great wealth transfer is coming, and women may emerge as the biggest beneficiaries. Approximately $30 trillion in wealth is set to change hands in the next three to four decades, and women are poised to inherit a sizable share from their spouses and aging parents.

Unfortunately, according to RBC Wealth Management's 2017 Wealth Transfer report, just 22% of women have a comprehensive wealth transfer plan in place.[11] We believe that using this book and connecting advisors and solution providers to women (and men) adds tremendous value at this critical juncture where the financial stakes are so high.

Question 3: Do you understand what the recommended components of a retirement plan are and how the right retirement strategies can impact your retirement outcome?

What the Research Says: A proper financial plan for retirement is more than a 401(k) plan or an investment strategy. As you'll find out in this retirement planning book, there are many facets of the plan that must be addressed and many strategies within a plan that must be considered. The components of your plan start out simple when you're many years from retirement, and they get a bit more complex as you get closer to retirement age. Retirement planning is part soul searching and part numbers crunching.

It starts with your financial and lifestyle goals and outlines how you'll use your assets and income in retirement to fulfill those goals…you'll need to do some soul searching here. Your goals may include working part-time, starting a business, volunteering, spending more time with family, pursuing a hobby, buying a second home, traveling, or relaxing.

Next comes the numbers-crunching part. The right retirement plan identifies all your projected retirement expenses and guaranteed income sources, and then identifies the gap between expenses and income. The gap is filled by your savings and assets and by turning them into an income stream for retirement. We call this a distribution strategy in which you'll be creating your retirement paycheck. The goal of your plan is to make your income (or distribution strategy) in retirement as efficient and sustainable as possible.

---

[9] Nasdaq, "Men vs. Women: Risk Aversion," November 6, 2013, www.nasdaq.com/article/men-vs-women-risk-aversion-cm297364.

[10] Rebecca Lake, "Women and the Great Wealth Transfer," *Investopedia*, June 25, 2019, https://www.investopedia.com/financial-advisor/women-and-great-wealth-transfer/.

[11] RBC Wealth Management, *Wealth Transfer Report*, 2017, https://www.rbcwealthmanagement.com/_global/static/documents/RBC-wealth-transfer-report-2017.pdf.

The right plan mitigates, to the greatest extent possible, the many risks you may face in retirement. These risks can potentially decimate an otherwise healthy portfolio. Amongst the major risks are longevity, volatility, sequence of return, inflation, portfolio overdraft/underdraft, interest rates, behavioral risk, and healthcare/long-term care. Because there are so many personal, political, and economic events we can't control in life and retirement, we need to outsmart these "what-ifs" with unconventional, yet effective and efficient strategies.

The right plan integrates research-backed income optimization and protection strategies that are more likely to help you live the retirement you've imagined. We call these Multi-Discipline Retirement Strategies (MDRS). These strategies include:

- ✓ Creating a balanced portfolio allocation of growth & guarantees
- ✓ Using active/passive portfolio management
- ✓ Optimizing Social Security timing
- ✓ Distributing income in a smart, tax-efficient manner
- ✓ Prudently using home equity
- ✓ Maximizing Medicare
- ✓ Protecting against long-term care
- ✓ Implementing insurance
- ✓ Establishing an estate plan

Recently, a number of companies have conducted research that assesses the impact of implementing proper retirement planning strategies on a retiree's financial future. This impact is measured in terms of Alpha. Adding Alpha to a retiree's plan adds significant value. If your advisor is providing great investment management services and comprehensive retirement planning, then you may be satisfied with the value you are receiving.

Vanguard Funds performed a study that concluded that proper retirement planning strategies can add as much as a 3% efficient yield or Alpha to a retirement portfolio.[12]

---

[12] David Van Knapp, "What Is the Value of An Advisor?" *Seeking Alpha*, February 13, 2017, https://seekingalpha.com/article/4045415-value-advisor-vanguard-totes-advisors-alpha.

I. Suitable asset allocation	> 0%
II. Cost-effective implementation	~ 0.45%
III. Rebalancing	~ 0.35%
IV. Behavioral coaching	~ 1.50%
V. Asset location	~ 0% - 0.75%
VI. Spending strategy (withdrawal order)	~ 0% - 0.70%
VII. Total-return investing	> 0%
Potential Value Added	"About 3%"

Here's a case study that shows the potential impact of deploying just a few of these Alpha strategies.

Creating Alpha Efficient Yield (AEY)

Inputs:
Married couple age 65 planning to retire at age 65   IRA Balance: $1,000,000.
Baseline Rate of Return (ROR) estimate: 5%
Retirement income generated from age 65-95: $30,000 per year / inflation-adjusted at 3%/yr

ALPHA EFFICIENT YIELD (AEY)	Total Income Generated (age 65-95)	Total Investment Account Balance (age 95)
0% AEY (traditional "investment-only" advisor)	$1,604,202.	$ 828,434.
1% AEY	$1,919,388.	$1,626,343.
2% AEY	$2,310,181.	$2,744,929.
3% AEY	$2,795,049.	$4,294,328.

As you see, a 3% or more additional Alpha Efficient Yield (AEY) is possible, inclusive of fees. When growing your assets, it's important to understand your portfolio Rate of Return (ROR). However, when in retirement it's important to understand that your ROR is the baseline portfolio return. By adding the effect of AEY, you have a much-improved potential for success. As the research indicates, working with a retirement advisor that can add AEY to your retirement portfolio can quite possibly be your biggest catalyst to a successful retirement. The case study below illustrates the dramatic difference and value this can add for a retiree.

In summary, the effect of Alpha Efficient Yield (AEY) can be significant. If an advisor employs Alpha Efficient retirement planning strategies in addition to their investment management, the average retiree can realize a huge difference.

Rather than living a "random retirement" where you ignore all these critical planning components and simply convert your 401(k) to an IRA and start withdrawing the monies to supplant your Social Security benefit, you can and should have an "intentional, calculated retirement" where you address each and every component, in writing, and then actually implement your plan with an advisor or on your own rather than just think about it.

> **"Those who have a written retirement plan have a nest egg 445% bigger than non-planners."** (HSBC, Future of Retirement, 2013)

Question 4: Do you understand the difference between retirement based on research vs. rhetoric?
What the Research Says: *"All too often we base our investment decisions on industry marketing and advertising or on what we read and hear in the media or on something else altogether."* (Robin Powell, financial journalist)[13]

We believe the best route to making reliable, data-driven decisions about your retirement (vs. best guesses or gut feel) is to open your mind and rely on research and analysis, cutting edge technology, and academically proven strategies. We call this science-based planning. Powerful and reliable. We're 100% committed to it (and you should be too)!

To this end, everything in this book is based on research provided by the leading retirement academics in the industry, not on what big insurance and investment company bigots with even bigger marketing budgets say. ALL your financial and retirement decisions should be based on research and data (not on what the TV commercials or your brother advise you to do)! Warren Buffet summed this up best with his quote, "You are neither right nor wrong because the crowd disagrees with you, you are right because your data and reasoning are right."[14]

Here is a list of some of the researchers whose expertise we base the content of this book on. We encourage you to follow their blogs and their research.

Moshe Milevsky, Ph.D.
Professor of finance at York University a leading authority on the intersection of wealth management, financial mathematics, and insurance

---

[13] "A Call for Kintsugi Portfolios," *Above the Market*, December 9, 2016, https://rpseawright.wordpress.com/2016/12/09/a-call-for-kintsugi-portfolios/.
[14] Joshua Kennon, "The Quotes and Wisdom of Warren Buffet," *The Balance*, May 1, 2020, https://www.thebalance.com/warren-buffett-quotes-356438.

Michael Finke, Ph.D.
Chief Academic Officer at The American College of Financial Services

David Blanchett, Ph.D., CFA, CFP
Head of retirement research at Morningstar and thought leader in the fields of wealth management and retirement

Jack Guttentag, Ph.D.
Professor emeritus of finance at the University of Pennsylvania and consumer advocate

Wade Pfau, Ph.D.
Professor of Retirement Income in the PhD in Financial and Retirement Planning program at The American College of Financial Services

Laurence Kotlikoff, Ph.D.
Professor of Economics at Boston University

Michael Kitces, CFP, CLU, ChFC, RHU, REBC & CASL
Financial planner, commentator, speaker, blogger, and educator

Roger Ibbotson, Ph.D.
Professor in the Practice Emeritus of Finance at Yale School of Management

Note: Proper retirement planning introduces many new ideas (and changes) to what you may have been doing with your money up to this point in your life, or what you've heard are the right things to do once you're in retirement. There are a glut of myths and misinformation in the financial services industry and many opinions (not unlike politics, religion, fitness, and nutrition). We suggest you embrace information from objective retirement experts and independent research rather than listen to the big marketing machines of investment and insurance conglomerates. The best we can suggest is to be open-minded to new ideas and opportunities. You may need an attitude adjustment and/or a significant change in behavior to improve your retirement outcome. Retirement introduces a whole new relationship with your money and how you think about it, manage it, control it, and make it last throughout your retirement. This platform is designed to help.

Question 5: Do you understand the importance of defining your goals for retirement: what you want to do in retirement, what lifestyle you want, where you want to live, and how you want to live?
What the Research Says: The number one question of retirees is, *When can I retire?* This book is designed to help you get knowledgeable about retirement. And it's also designed to help you determine this by helping you take an inventory of *what* you've got, identifying *where* your gaps are, providing research-based ideas on *how* to fill the gaps, and then creating and implementing a financially efficient and sustainable plan.

Make sure you know where you are today and where you want to be tomorrow...define your lifestyle goals and then map those to your financial goals. Some people are afraid to see what they have and prefer to bury their heads in the sand and hope for the best. This strategy never got anyone anywhere except deeper in the hole. The best strategy is to look reality in the face and deal with it...the good, the bad, and the ugly.

Question 6: Do you understand the difference between the accumulation phase of life and the distribution phase of life?
What the Research Says: The accumulation phase of life is the time before retirement (say, when you are 20–50 years old). The accumulation period is where you want to make smart decisions about how to save for retirement, but also live a good life. The accumulation phase has a different set of money rules than the distribution phase of life. During accumulation, time is on your side so you can be more aggressive with your portfolio, as you have time to recover from market dips. The effect of compound interest is also on your side so it's easier to save more the sooner you start. In the distribution phase of life, which kicks in once you retire, you'll be drawing from your savings and assets, and counting on a retirement paycheck, in addition to your income sources such as pensions, 401(k)s, and Social Security.

Making sure your money lasts in retirement requires many more considerations and strategies. There's also a period between Accumulation and Distribution called Transition. This period is about 5–10 years prior to your desired retirement date, and it is when you need to seriously start preparing yourself mentally and financially for retirement. A transition period is helpful because it allows you time to make sure you're preparing properly. Accumulation is about growth. Transition is about preparation and initial changes in your strategy (i.e. portfolio allocation) and Distribution is about efficiency, safety, and some guarded growth.

Retirement Risks

Question 7: Do you understand the impact of longevity risk on your retirement?
What the Research Says: Longevity risk is the chance you will live a very long life, which is a good thing (assuming you stay relatively healthy and alert). With increased life expectancy, however, your portfolio must last longer. You must prepare for 20–30 years or longer in retirement. The average 65-year-old American can expect to live another 19.4 years. For married couples who reach age 65, there's a 50% chance one spouse will live to 92 and a 25% chance one will live to 97. And it's expected that life expectancy will continue to increase. This is perhaps the most important risk you must account for in your retirement plan.

Question 8: Do you understand the impact of volatility risk on your retirement?

What the Research Says: Volatility is a statistical measure of the dispersion of returns for a given security or market index. Commonly, the higher the volatility, the riskier the security (Investopedia, 2017).[15] A recent study completed by Sure Dividend, *Why You Must Care About Volatility in Retirement* concluded, "Simply put, the greater the volatility of your portfolio, the greater chance you have of outliving your money all other things being equal. By its nature, higher volatility means greater swings in the value of your portfolio."[16] In the growth phase, when you're accumulating your assets, volatility has virtually no effect on the final value of a growth portfolio. In the income distribution phase, when taking income from your assets, volatility has a major effect on a portfolio when taking withdrawals.

As an example, here's a look at how two traditional portfolios performed over a 20-year period ending 2017: one conservative and one aggressive. During the best year, the conservative portfolio (50% stocks/30% bonds/20% cash alternatives) would have earned almost 17%. During its worst year, it would have *lost* more than 13%. The average annual return was approximately 6%.

The aggressive portfolio (75% stock/25% bonds/5% cash alternatives), on the other hand, would have earned about 24.5% during the best year and would have *lost* more than 30% during the worst year! The average annual return over this period was about 7%. This shows how an aggressive portfolio is more susceptible to volatility.

Note: This example is used for illustrative purposes only. The returns shown do not include taxes, fees, and other expenses typically associated with investing. The performance of an unmanaged index is not indicative of the performance of any particular investment. Individuals cannot invest directly in an index. Past performance is not indicative of future results. Actual results will vary. Source: Thomson Reuters, 2018.[17] Performance described is for the period January 1, 1998, to December 31, 2017. Stocks are represented by the S&P 500 composite total return index, bonds are represented by the Citigroup Corporate Bond Composite Index, and cash alternatives are represented by the Citigroup Three-Month Treasury Bill Index. Each of these indexes is generally considered representative of its respective asset classes. T-bills are backed by the full faith and credit of the U.S. government as to the timely payment of principal and interest. The return and principal value of stock and bond investments fluctuate with changes in market conditions. When sold, these securities may be worth more or less than the original amount invested.

---

[15] Justin Kuepper, "Volatility Definition," Investopedia, March 13, 2020, https://www.investopedia.com/terms/v/volatility.asp.

[16] Sure Dividend, "Why You Must Care About Volatility in Retirement," *Seeking Alpha*, October 14, 2014, https://seekingalpha.com/article/2560525-why-you-must-care-about-volatility-in-retirement?page=2).

[17] Broadridge Investor Communications Solutions, *Investment Fundamentals: Five Myths and Truths of Investing*, 2018, https://www.broadridgeadvisor.com/docs/seminar/investment-fundamentals-workbook.pdf.

Question 9: Do you understand the impact of sequence of return risk on your retirement?
What the Research Says: A similar risk to volatility, sequence of return risk is the risk of receiving lower or negative returns early in a period when withdrawals are made from investments (Investopedia, 2017).[18] The first 10 years of returns will indicate your retirement outcome. A negative sequence equals lower returns in the early years of retirement. A positive sequence equals higher than average returns in the early years. Because you don't know what sequence you will retire into, it's imperative to run income projections in negative, average, and positive sequences of return markets.

As an example, a 25% negative single-year return in a retirement portfolio will have the biggest impact on long-term retirement security if it occurs at retirement. Significant negative returns occurring at or near retirement have a much bigger impact on whether portfolio withdrawals will be sustainable throughout retirement than if they occur well before or well after the retirement date.

While the sequence of return risk cannot be controlled any more than market volatility, its effect can be mitigated. The primary strategy for addressing this risk is to reduce portfolio risk—especially during the 5-year period prior to and after retirement. Reducing risk can mean reducing the allocation to stocks and moving toward structured investments and fixed indexed annuities.

Having a "safe money" bucket of funds to draw income from in the event of a dramatic downturn in the stock market can be an effective strategy to protect the portfolio from a negative sequence of return risk. Research studies have concluded that having this "buffer" to draw from when market losses occur can have a positive effect on the long-term survivability of the overall portfolio.

A major psychological benefit of the income buffer strategy is that it will enable retirees to withstand the temptation to exit the stock market with their retirement funds during a period of market losses, possibly putting the retiree in a market timing guessing game. Such an approach often leads to selling at the market low and buying at the market high, and dramatically underperforming a long-term buy and hold strategy. Numerous studies have shown that the average investor has dramatically underperformed the market returns due to irrational selling and buying decisions.

As an example, during the 2007–2008 stock market downturn, having a safe money buffer or reserve account to withdraw income from (until the stock portion of the portfolio rebounded)

---

[18] Julia Kagan, "Sequence Risk," *Investopedia*, July 31, 2019, https://www.investopedia.com/terms/s/sequence-risk.asp.

would have been a positive step to protect against a negative sequence of return risk. As a reference, in an article dated February 2015 by Wealthfront's Andy Rachleff and Duncan Gilchrist, Ph.D., the 2007–2009 market loss was 56.39% and it took the market 1,485 days or 4.06 years to recover.[19] Since 1911, the average recovery time after a stock market downturn has been 684 days or 1.87 years! Based on this fact, it's prudent to have a buffer in place three to five years before retirement begins, and it should cover approximately four to five years of retirement income. A proper buffer can consist of life insurance cash values, a reverse mortgage reserve account, cash or CDs, a guaranteed annuity, or any other account that will have a limited effect when there is a stock market downturn.

Question 10: Do you understand the impact of inflation risk on your retirement?
What the Research Says: Inflation is the rate at which the prices of goods and services rise. Inflation has a major effect on the entire country's economy. It impacts not only the government, but also the little things in the average person's daily life, and it can have a big impact on your retirement.

Just as a quick example, let's say a retiree begins retirement on a total income of $3,000 per month, that same retiree would need $5,432 per month in 20 years at a 3% inflation rate just to maintain the same standard of income. To put it another way, a loaf of bread that costs $3.00 today would cost $5.00 at a 3% inflationary increase over a 20-year period.

Historically, inflation has averaged 3%. Most prudent income projections should incorporate a 3% inflation rate. However, you could adjust the rate down to 2% to mimic what is referred to as income smoothing. The idea of income smoothing is that spending as you enter the middle and end of retirement goes down. Therefore, you won't need as much income. By decreasing inflation by 1% you can mimic the effects of income smoothing.

What is a retiree to do to combat these risks of longevity, volatility, sequence of return, and inflation? The only asset that has historically outpaced inflation has been stocks. The downside to stocks is that they are typically extremely volatile and risky on a year-by-year basis, and you could retire into a negative sequence of return market. Any long-term retirement planning strategy must include a diversified portfolio of stocks to help reduce the effects of inflation and the effect of longevity risk, while also having some type of risk control measures or income guarantees to reduce risk and volatility.

---

[19] Andy Rachleff and Duncan Gilchrist, "Stock Market Corrections: Not as Scary as You Think," *Wealthfront*, February 2015, https://blog.wealthfront.com/stock-market-corrections-not-as-scary-as-you-think/.

Question 11: Do you understand the impact of Portfolio Overdraft or Underdraft risk?
What the Research Says: Portfolio Overdraft risk is a term we've coined to describe the real risk of taking too much money out of your portfolio. 61% of people fear outliving their income more than they fear death. Taking too much money too soon is frightening to both those who have saved prudently, as well as those who feel behind. It's critical not to randomize your withdrawal amounts in retirement (taking too much or too little). There are rules of thumb to determine the proper (safe) withdrawal amounts, as well as the most appropriate methods to begin distributing monies from your portfolio. See question 39 for more details.

Question 12: Do you understand the impact of taxes on your retirement?
What the Research Says: Many people have no idea the impact taxes can have on retirement. Nor do they know how to distribute their assets tax-efficiently once in retirement. Why give Uncle Sam more than we need to? Taxes are a complex topic, it's best to have a qualified advisor create a tax plan for your retirement. Doing so can potentially add 10–15 years or more to your portfolio survival.
We recommend the Five Bucket Tax Strategy for tax planning, which includes:
1. Taxable bucket (any accounts that you pay taxes on each year, regardless of whether you pull money out, including CDs, mutual funds, stock dividends, and anything that generates a 1099)
2. Tax-deferred bucket (qualified retirement plans: 401(k)s, 403bs, 457s, IRAs, non-qualified annuities, and savings bonds)
3. Tax-free bucket (Roth IRAs, municipal bonds, and properly structured life insurance)
4. Income and estate tax-free bucket (charitable trusts)
5. Triple tax-free bucket (Health Savings Accounts or HSAs)
   HSAs are a newer tax-advantaged vehicle few people realize can have a great impact on their retirement. It offers tax-deductible contributions, tax-deferred growth, and tax-free withdrawals for qualified health care expenses (a potentially smart strategy for healthcare costs and lowering taxes). Hence, the moniker – triple tax-free.

A retirement advisor who is well versed in retirement tax planning can help you determine your Five Bucket Tax Strategy and how to position your assets tax-efficiently in each bucket. Your advisor will then help you determine how to start withdrawing from each of these buckets for an efficient and sustainable income for life. See more information in the Tax section of this summary.

Question 13: Do you understand the impact of interest rate risk on your retirement?
What the Research Says: Interest rate risk is the potential for rising interest rates to cause a decrease in the price of an investment. When interest rates go up, the current market price of bonds goes down.

As an example, an interest rate rise of 1% will cause a 10-year duration bond to decline by approximately 10% in value. From a historical perspective, current interest rates are at the lowest levels we've seen in over 50 years. Historically, safe, high-quality US government and corporate bonds have returned 5–6%, which in this low-interest-rate environment will be impossible to find. In addition, "safe" bonds are susceptible to substantial losses when interest rates rise.

Research proves the point that in a generally increasing interest rate environment, our safe money bonds will suffer far lower overall returns than when the interest rate environment is generally falling (Morningstar Advisor Workstation, Release date 06-30-2017).[20]

In conclusion, investors expecting bond funds to perform as well in the next ten years as they have in the last ten will be disappointed. As previously discussed, bonds can play an important role in retirement portfolios, reducing volatility and increasing the predictability of returns. However, the stellar performance of bonds from 1982 through 2017 (decreasing interest rate environment) will not be repeated anytime soon. In fact, there is even the risk of *negative* returns. In the current low-interest-rate environment (5-year treasury yield is 1.736% and the 10-year yield is 1.921, according to CNBC.com as of 11/11/19), it's imperative to find a safe alternative or accept much lower overall portfolio returns.[21] Another alternative is to use a far more aggressive portfolio mix and accept greater volatility. This strategy, however, can be detrimental to the survivability of a portfolio when taking withdrawals.

Question 14: Do you understand the impact of behavioral risk on your retirement?
What the Research Says: This risk relates to how people make financial decisions and the biases that can handicap their decision-making. Behavioral finance is a field of research that combines psychology and economics to try to understand how and why people make decisions that are not always economically rational. It looks at our natural biases—including the tendencies toward inertia in decision-making, discounting the future, irrational behavior, and the aversion to loss—all in an effort to see how they affect our financial decisions.

Many investors have the temptation to chase returns and make uninformed, knee-jerk reactions as volatile markets move up and down. In fact, these behaviors have been proven in numerous studies to negatively impact portfolios over the long term. In a 2014 Quantitative Analysis of Investor Behavior survey by Dalbar, it was shown that investors' propensity to buy at market peaks and sell at market lows resulted in average individual investor returns of 2.5%

---

[20] Morningstar® Advisor Workstation℠ Morningstar Analysis Snapshot Report, June 23, 2017.
[21] Sam Meredith, Yun Li, "Treasury Yields Fall Slightly as US-China Trade Remains in Focus," CNBC.com, November 19, 2019, https://www.cnbc.com/2019/11/19/us-bonds-wall-street-in-focus-as-us-china-trade-deal-doubts-persist.html.

over a 20-year period vs. the S&P of 9.2%.[22] Consumers don't always act in ways that are consistent with their self-interest, which poses a risk to retirement security. A steady hand during turbulent times, like that offered by a retirement advisor, can have a significant impact on the long-term survivability of your portfolio.

Question 15: Do you understand the impact of health care/long-term care risk on your retirement?

What the Research Says: Many people underestimate the potential cost of healthcare in retirement, forgetting the premiums, copays, deductibles, and prescription drugs they might have to cover—even with Medicare, which typically covers approximately 60% of the average retiree's healthcare costs. How much could you spend on healthcare in retirement?

If Medicare benefits remain unchanged, it's estimated that a 65-year-old married couple might need $296,000 to cover health care alone during a 25-year retirement (source: Bank of America, 2019 Workplace Benefits Report).[23] A single man can expect to spend $148,000, while a woman can expect to spend $161,000. Those with chronic illnesses will spend more than those who go in only for routine checkups, but even routine care can be expensive over the years.

Consider that medical costs could be even higher for those with chronic illnesses or high-cost prescription drug needs. And other costs, such as dental expenses, glasses, and hearing aids for those who need them aren't captured in these figures.

Another health-related risk many retirees eventually face is the need for long-term care. Long-term care refers to the assistance needed to manage a chronic illness, disability, or cognitive impairment that leaves you unable to care for yourself for an extended period. It includes nursing home care, as well as care provided in an assisted-living facility, adult day-care center, or even at home. The statistics surrounding long-term care can be scary. Consider that

- More than half of people over age 65 will need some form of long-term care during their lifetimes.
- Currently, the average annual cost of a semi-private room in a nursing home is $82,128, and in many states, the actual cost is much higher.
- If costs rise at just 3% a year (a conservative estimate), a one-year stay in a nursing home would top $149,000 in 20 years.

---

[22] Dalbar, *20th Annual Quantitative Analysis of Investor Behavior 2014 Advisor Edition*, http://kyestates.com/wp-content/uploads/2015/02/DALBAR-QAIB-2014.pdf.

[23] Bank of America, *2019 Workplace Benefits Report: Expanding the Financial Wellness Conversation*, https://www.benefitplans.baml.com/publish/content/application/pdf/GWMOL/2019WorkplaceBenefitsReport.pdf.

Unfortunately, Medicare and traditional medical insurance offer little or no relief for this type of care. And if you qualify for Medicaid by spending down your assets, it typically means you lose some control over where you receive care and, subsequently, the type of care offered (source: U.S. Department of Health and Human Services, 2018).[24] Cost projection is a hypothetical example of mathematical principles and is used for illustrative purposes only. Actual results will vary.

It's critical to calculate the right costs of health care, long-term care needs, and insurance into your retirement income projection. Without proper risk management strategies and accounting for these costs, either could decimate a healthy portfolio.

The best defense against healthcare costs is to prioritize a healthy lifestyle, including nutrition, exercise, and mental wellness.

Debt

Question 16: Do you understand the impact of revolving debt and the need to reduce it prior to retirement?

What the Research Says: Debt reduction, such as bad debt like revolving credit, is at any time an important financial goal. Reducing bad debt prior to retirement is critical. Next in line is reducing other debts with fixed rates and payments, such as a mortgage or auto loan. Those are more predictable, and therefore easier to plan for as part of a retirement budget, but they can still be worth chipping away at, so you have fewer expenses in retirement. According to a report from the Transamerica Center for Retirement Studies, four in ten retirees cite "paying off debt" as a current financial priority—putting it on equal footing with "just getting by to cover basic living expenses" as a top concern. Almost three in ten cite paying down credit card debt as a priority, while 17% are focusing on mortgage debt and 11% on some other consumer debt, such as medical bills or student loans. Among those with mortgage debt, 9% owe more than $100,000. Taking steps to reduce and manage debt ahead of retirement can lessen the burden on your income in retirement.[25]

---

[24] Medicare.gov, https://www.medicare.gov/your-medicare-costs/get-help-paying-costs/medicaid.
[25] Transamerica Center for Retirement Studies, "How You Manage Debt Will Impact Those Retirement Dreams," https://umf.org/personal-finance/2019/5/8/how-you-manage-debt-will-impact-those-retirement-dreams.

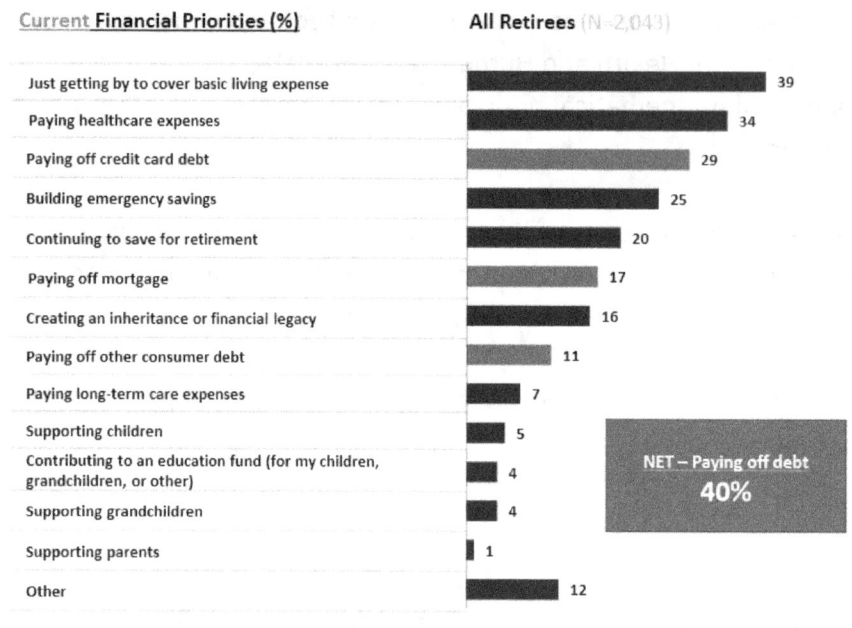

If it looks like you'll retire with some debt, factor that repayment into your overall plan and income projection analysis. Your retirement plan should also include saving for anticipated big-ticket purchases or expenses in retirement (such as a roof on your house, a new car, or a medical emergency). This way you won't have to pull these monies from a retirement account (which could trigger a tax event) or take on substantial new debt. You want to try to avoid new, late-career, or early-retirement debt.

Question 17: Do you understand the impact of paying off your mortgage prior to retirement?
What the Research Says: Reducing housing debt is important if you plan to use your home's equity as an income buffer in retirement. Many people choose to speed up their mortgage payments on their homes prior to retirement. This strategy and decision should be incorporated into your overall "transition" plan and the "where you want to live" question. It's also a component of your overall retirement income projection. You can read more about this in the Reverse Mortgage section.

Question 18: Do you understand the impact of the car and recreational vehicle loan expenses in retirement?
What the Research Says: While we are probably going to be driving around for many years in retirement (or perhaps we'll just be passengers in a self-driving auto), some people choose to

downsize their BMW to a Kia…not a bad decision given Kia's outstanding reputation for value by the way.

Perhaps in retirement, you and your spouse no longer need two cars and the sports car or motorcycles in the garage. Perhaps you will live in a community of golf carts or in Holland where everyone rides a bike! Downsizing car loan debt (and expenses) is a good practical step to take in retirement. Unless of course, your lifestyle goal includes cruising around in the Mustang Shelby 350. We may not blame you…that's one way to feel forever young. Just be prepared for the expense and watch the speeding tickets.

Income in Retirement

Question 19: Do you understand the need to calculate your monthly net income in retirement (known as a retirement income projection), adjusting for annual inflation of 2–3%?
What the Research Says: The number one fear for pre-retirees is running out of money in retirement (source: Allianz Life Insurance Survey, 2010).[26] Yet, 81% of people don't know how much income they need to retire (source: New Challenges, New Solutions, 2017).[27] How much one needs depends on how much they have saved and what lifestyle they wish to support.

You've likely heard the conventional wisdom that says you should aim to have a nest egg of $1 million to $1.5 million saved as you enter retirement. Or that your savings should amount to 10 to 12 times your current income to generate an income for life. There is no way of knowing what will happen to interest rates and inflation in the future, but for a retiree to generate a $40,000 a year "retirement paycheck" after stopping work, he or she will need savings of about $1.18 million to support a 30-year retirement. This was calculated using average returns of 6% and inflation at 2.5%, according to Morningstar, a Chicago-based investment-research firm.[28]

Before you panic about this number (or give up trying to reach it), this "magic number" is different for everyone and there are some very unique strategies you can deploy to make what you have as efficient as possible without adding a single cent to what you've saved.

A proper retirement planning process accounts for all your guaranteed income sources including pensions, Social Security, reverse mortgage, and income from annuities. Here is a breakdown of the typical income sources for retirees.

---

[26] Allianz Life Insurance Company, "Outliving Your Money Feared More Than Death."
[27] Tom Anderson, "81% of Americans Don't Know How Much They Need to Retire," CNBC.com, February 15, 2017, https://www.cnbc.com/2017/02/15/80-of-americans-dont-know-how-much-they-need-to-retire.html.
[28] Carolyn O'Hara, "How Much Money Do I Need to Retire?" AARP.org, https://www.aarp.org/work/retirement-planning/info-2015/nest-egg-retirement-amount.html.

Equivalized Household Income Deciles for Households Headed by a Person Aged 65 or Over: 2017

(Amounts in 2017 dollars)

Decile	Lower limit	Upper limit (less than)
1	Z	12,640
2	12,640	18,310
3	18,310	23,390
4	23,390	28,970
5	28,970	34,900
6	34,900	41,660
7	41,660	50,680
8	50,680	62,630
9	62,630	85,390
10	85,390	D

D Withheld to avoid disclosure.
Z Represents or rounds to zero.
Source: U.S. Census Bureau, 2018 Survey of Income and Program Participation.

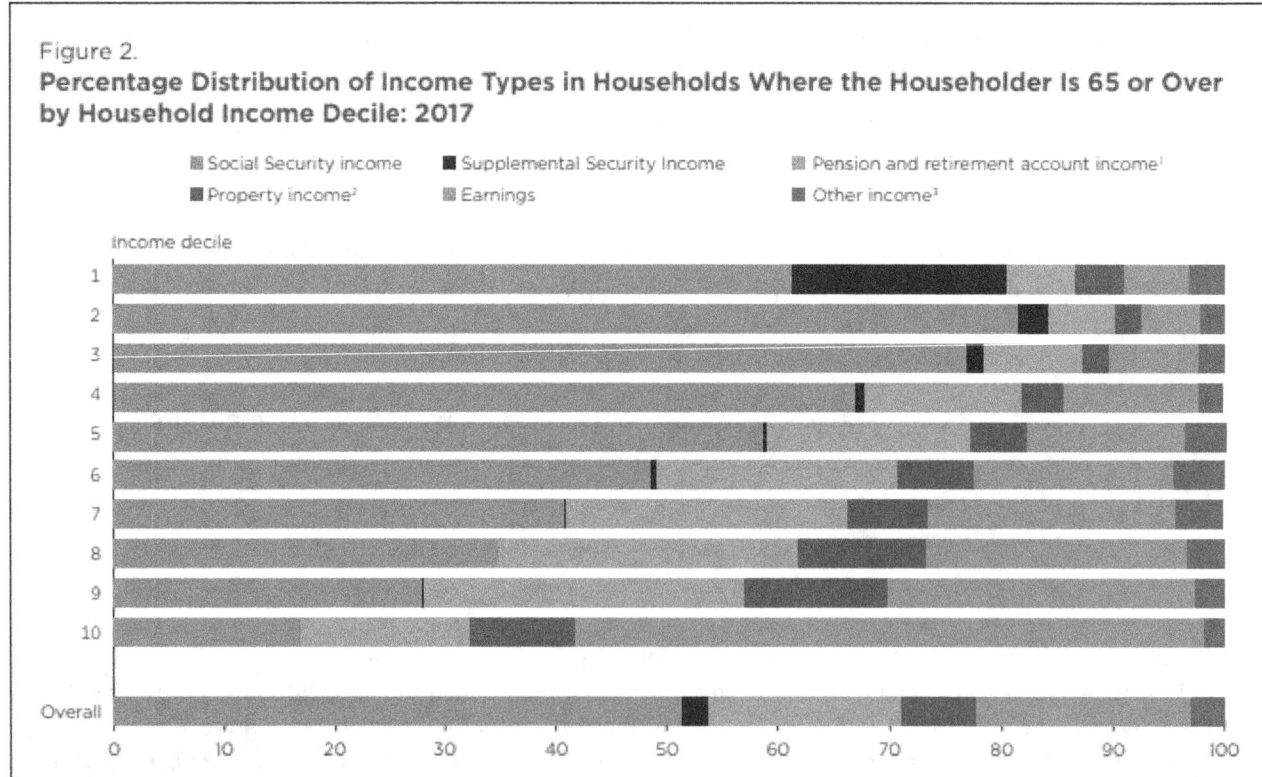

Figure 2.
Percentage Distribution of Income Types in Households Where the Householder Is 65 or Over by Household Income Decile: 2017

[1] Includes retirement, disability, survivor, life insurance, and annuity income.
[2] Includes income from interest, dividends, rents, and other assets held outside of retirement accounts.
[3] Includes unemployment compensation, workers' compensation, veterans' payments, and other cash income sources.
Source: U.S. Census Bureau, 2018 Survey of Income and Program Participation.

As you can see, on average Social Security alone will account for over half of your income sources, with your earnings accounting for less than a third. Note, however, that roughly 60% of workers had to stop working before they intended to due to reasons such as layoffs or health issues, according to a 2015 study by Voya Financial. So, earnings can be planned, but are not always guaranteed. Therefore, we should count only Social Security, pensions, annuities, and reverse mortgages as guaranteed income sources.

The next step in your retirement income planning will be to determine expenses. You'll then determine your gap between expenses and guaranteed income sources. With your gap identified you'll calculate how your savings and investments, including things like your 401(k), can be turned into a retirement paycheck to fill your gap.

The ultimate goal of proper income planning is to detail your Income Optimization and Distribution strategies to make sure you don't outlive your money. It also includes a retirement income projection, or what we call our Retirement Efficiency Assessment, which provides a calculation of the income you'll need in retirement to support your lifestyle, taking into account inflationary factors, typically 2–3%. This projection must include all your variables, expenses, risks, etc.

Question 20: Do you understand the strategies for maximizing pension benefits for your household?

What the Research Says: If you're entitled to receive a traditional pension from an employer-sponsored pension plan, you're lucky. Fewer Americans are covered by such plans every year. For example, in 1998, 59% of Fortune 500 companies offered a defined benefit plan or pension. By 2017, that figure had dropped to 16%.[29]

When it's time to start your pension, you need to make a number of decisions. If you haven't already selected a payout option, you'll want to carefully consider your choices. Generally, your retirement benefit is an annuity, payable over your lifetime, beginning at the plan's normal retirement age (typically age 65). Many plans allow you to retire earlier but will actuarially adjust your benefit to account for the fact that payments begin sooner and will last for a longer period of time. The options that are right for you depend on your individual situation, including your (and your spouse's) age, health, and other financial resources.

Make sure that you completely understand all your options before you decide. You'll also want to make sure that you know whether your pension benefit will be adjusted periodically for inflation. Prior to retirement, your pension plan will provide you with an explanation of all your options and the relative values of any optional forms of benefits available to you. Be sure to read through this document carefully.

---

[29] Barney, "A Mere 16% of Fortune 500 Companies Offer a DB Plan."

Question 21: Do you understand the role annuities play as a guaranteed income source?
What the Research Says: There are two types of annuities:

1. Immediate Income Annuity, in which you typically must turn on the income benefit within 12 months. This is known as a Single Premium Immediate Annuity (SPIA).
2. Accumulation or growth annuity, in which you allow the value to accumulate over time, eventually taking income as needed at some future date. You typically will use a systematic withdrawal income plan (SWIP). For purposes of calculating your guaranteed income sources, you will include an immediate annuity in this calculation.

A Single Premium Immediate Annuity (SPIA) has two different purchase options: purchase with a lump sum payment (non-qualified or qualified) or convert any annuity from accumulation to an SPIA. Your guaranteed income payout options include:

- Lifetime income
- Lifetime Income with 10-year and 20-year certainty
- Lifetime income with survivor options, plus, many more options

Income annuities can be a great guaranteed income source eliminating longevity risk.

Question 22: Do you understand the importance of calculating your monthly expenses in retirement?
What the Research Says: Retirement expenses can certainly go down in retirement, but it's best to use an expense worksheet, Excel spreadsheet, or another tool to list and categorize all your expected expenses in retirement. Some experts suggest that expenses in retirement are 60–80% of pre-retirement expenses. Others suggest planning on 100% of your pre-retirement income each year for at least the first 10 years after you stop working. The belief is that your spending really won't slow down in early retirement (what is referred to as the "go-go" years of retirement). As you enter the "slow-go" and eventually "no-go" years, expenses should decline. But these are just guidelines.

Some expenses, like housing, may go down in retirement, while others such as health care and travel may increase. Many people overlook the cost of healthcare and long-term care in their expense projections. Creating a detailed retirement budget is a valuable exercise.

Question 23: Do you understand the importance of identifying the gap between your expenses and guaranteed income sources and filling the gap with other income sources and/or your savings and investments?
What the Research Says: Knowing your gap is critical. Although it might be more than you'd like, it's the basis of your income distribution strategy moving forward. You'll fill the gap with your "other sources" of income and/or savings and investments. These include 401(k)/403bs, traditional and Roth Individual Retirement Accounts (IRAs), annuities, bonds, mutual funds,

certificates of deposit, employment income, inheritances, life insurance, and rental real estate. Each one offers a different set of strategies to optimize for retirement.

Question 24: Do you understand the other methods to fill your gap?
What the Research Says: There are a number of things you can do to close any gap you're facing. These include:
- Savvy savers could double, on average, their nest eggs in the last 10 years of their working years, thanks to the magic of compound interest. If the market delivers its historical average of 7% annually, your money will double every decade. You could also make a dent in your expenses by being budget conscious and reducing extraneous expenses to add to your savings.

The chart below highlights the value of starting to save early and staying consistent.

Age you start saving for retirement	Save $2,000 per year	Save $5,000 per year	Save $10,000 per year
	at age 65, you'll have...		
20	$425,487	$1,063,718	$2,127,435
30	$222,870	$557,174	$1,114,348
40	$109,729	$274,323	$548,645
50	$46,552	$116,380	$232,760
60	$11,274	$28,185	$56,371

- Time allowing, you can increase your assets by saving more and continuing to pursue investment growth.
- Modify your lifestyle to make ends meet.
- Consider downsizing.
- Review your debt. Can you pay off or consolidate debt to reduce your monthly interest costs?
- Retiring doesn't mean you have to stop working all at once. Talk to your employer about a phased retirement. Shift down in hours and responsibilities over a multi-year period.
- Consider working part-time in retirement or finding a passive income stream. You'll earn extra income and you may have less time available to spend money.
    - There's nothing like the power of an income to power your retirement savings.
        - If you plan to fall back on continued employment during retirement, consider that many retirees leave work earlier than planned due to health issues or other unforeseen circumstances, such as a layoff. A 2019 Employee Benefits

Research Institute report revealed that 8 in 10 workers think they will work for pay in retirement, when, based on retiree experiences, only 28% actually do. In addition, workers are even more likely to expect that working for pay will be a source of income—74% of workers expect there to be at least a minor source of income in retirement.[30]

- Also keep in mind that if you claim Social Security benefits before reaching full retirement age and continue to work, your benefits will be reduced if your earnings exceed certain limits. And regardless of when you claim benefits, if you earn more than a certain amount, your Social Security benefits could become taxable, up to certain limits.

Of course, working for pay should always be an option to consider. Just remember that there's a lot to think about when it comes to working in retirement.

Question 25: Do you understand how to protect a surviving spouse from loss of income?
What the Research Says: There are specific steps that you'll need to take to make sure that the surviving spouse does not suffer from loss of income in the case of the death of one of the spouses. Your advisor can provide guidance on joint survivorship benefits.

Here are five ways to protect a surviving spouse in retirement:
1. **Maximize the Social Security spousal benefit**
   When a surviving spouse is at least 60 years old he/she is entitled to a survivor's benefit based on the Social Security record of the deceased spouse. Survivor benefits can be as much as 100% of the benefit received by the deceased spouse. If the surviving spouse claims the benefit before reaching full retirement age, the benefit will be decreased by up to 28.5%. The amount of the survivor's benefit is dependent on the amount of the deceased spouse's benefit. Because of the importance of survivor benefits, it's important to make sure both spouses make the right decisions regarding their claiming strategy.

2. **Widowhood plan**
   Premature death of one spouse can negatively impact retirement income. The impact is especially significant if the couple depends heavily on a pension or annuity without regard for survivor benefits. In the case of both spouses receiving Social Security, the death of one spouse will cause a loss of total benefits. The surviving spouse will receive the higher of the two benefit monthly payments. To prepare for this, a widowhood plan should be in place for the surviving spouse. This can be in the form of life insurance to replace income, a reverse mortgage, or downsizing your lifestyle to reduce expenses.

---

[30] Employee Benefit Research Institute, *2019 Retirement Confidence Survey Summary Report*, April 23, 2019, https://www.ebri.org/docs/default-source/rcs/2019-rcs/2019-rcs-short-report.pdf.

3. **Long-term care plan**
   A long-term care event can surely decimate a retirement portfolio. It's important for couples to consider how to protect a portfolio so that an event doesn't make a surviving spouse vulnerable to running out of money in the remainder of his/her retirement years. A long-term care insurance policy or saving for long-term care is prudent in this case.

4. **Death expense plan**
   It's not enough that one must deal with the emotional loss of a spouse, but death comes with a plethora of expenses. These include debts, medical bills, funeral expenses, probate costs, taxes, and the financial cost of making distributions to heirs. Not planning for these expenses with a reserve fund could result in having to tap hard assets. You can and should plan ahead, either through savings or insurance plans, to aid the surviving spouse in dealing with not just the emotional concerns, but also the financial issues.

5. **Creditor asset protection plan**
   Many things in life can put your assets at risk: dissatisfied clients, a business that goes bust, or a customer lawsuit against your business. If you could potentially be presented with these types of events and obligations to creditors, you will want to protect any potential negative impact on your spouse and their portfolio. An easy way to protect your assets is to make sure you title them correctly. Several states recognize a marital property ownership type known as tenancy by the entirety. Tenancy by entirety makes it difficult for a creditor of one spouse to collect a judgment from jointly owned property.
   You should seek the advice of an estate planning lawyer about using this strategy to protect your spouse in the event of your death.

The right plan prioritizes protecting the livelihood of a surviving spouse from life's what-ifs.

Question 26: Do you understand that in order to maximize your lifelong Social Security income, you need to choose the optimal time to begin benefits (and there definitely is an optimal time and it varies by person and circumstance)?

What the Research Says: One of the greatest concerns of retirees and near-retirees is the fear of outliving their assets. Although traditional pensions once provided a steady income for many retirees, the number of companies offering such plans has declined dramatically. Social Security typically represents about 33% of a retiree's income in retirement so it's important to get your filing strategy and timing correct. Below, you will find a breakdown of benefits as of January 2023.

Social Security offers benefits that are like a pension, plus a lot more. Not only does it provide a guaranteed income stream, but it also offers longevity protection, spousal protection, and even some inflation protection. Yet the ultimate value of Social Security benefits is often overlooked. For example, did you know that if you delay claiming benefits past full retirement age, you could increase your payments by as much as 8% a year? It would be hard to find a risk-free investment that currently offers that kind of payout.

However, the "When to begin benefits?" decision is different for everyone, is not always beyond your full retirement age, and must be incorporated into an overall retirement income projection analysis.

Generally, the earliest age to claim benefits is 62. (Surviving spouses, however, can claim survivor benefits as early as age 60.) "Full retirement age" ranges from 66 to 67, depending on the year of birth. You can receive your maximum monthly benefit by waiting until age 70 to claim Social Security.

While Social Security calculators can help point you in the right direction on claiming your benefit, they don't incorporate your entire income scenario and very important tax implications, which can impact your decisions.

Whether you're single, married, divorced, or widowed, there are strategies that might increase the monthly and lifetime Social Security benefits you receive. We want you to understand your claiming options and avoid costly mistakes that could reduce the Social Security income that you, and possibly your spouse, receive.

Type of beneficiary	Percent of total payouts	Average monthly benefit
All recipients	100%	$1,536.94
Retirement benefits	77.0%	$1,618.29
Retired workers	72.7%	$1,665.18
Survivor benefits	9.0%	$1,325.68
Nondisabled widow(er)s	5.4%	$1,559.42
Disability insurance	14.0%	$1,224.53
Disabled workers	12.0%	$1,360.16

Source: Social Security Administration, March 2022

Question 27: Do you understand the Social Security spousal strategy & how it could potentially increase your household's income?
What the Research Says: Even if you've never worked under Social Security, you may be able to

claim spousal retirement benefits if you are at least 62 years of age and your spouse is receiving retirement or disability benefits. You can also qualify for Medicare at age 65. If you are divorced, you may still be able to get benefits on your ex-spouse's record.

Married individuals are eligible to receive a Social Security benefit based on their own earnings history or a spousal benefit based on the spouse's primary insurance amount. (This is also true for unmarried, divorced individuals who were married for at least 10 years.)

If you're married, you can claim a spousal benefit whether or not you have worked. But to qualify for the spousal benefit, you must be at least age 62, you must have been married for at least one year, and your spouse must have filed for Social Security benefits. (An eligible, unmarried divorced spouse does not have to wait until his or her ex files for benefits, but the ex must be at least age 62.)

If you elect to receive a spousal benefit *before* you reach full retirement age, you will receive a permanently reduced amount, unless you are caring for a qualifying child. The benefit reduction is based on *your* age when you claim the spousal benefit. If you claim the spousal benefit upon reaching *your* full retirement age, the benefit would be one-half of your spouse's primary insurance amount (PIA).

The spousal benefit is never higher than 50% of the primary worker's full benefit. So, for example, if your spouse's primary insurance amount is $2,400, you could receive a $1,200 monthly spousal benefit by claiming it at your full retirement age.

Keep in mind that there are many combinations for how a married couple can claim Social Security retirement benefits and spousal benefits as well as other filing strategies. In fact, according to the Social Security Administration, the claiming-age combinations that married couples might choose can range from nearly 10,000 to 40,000, depending on their respective birth years.

Rather than rely only on a Social Security calculator, it's highly recommended that you speak to a retirement planner who is skilled in Social Security strategies to make sure you and your spouse understand how to use the spousal benefit correctly and make the right claiming decisions.

Question 28: Do you understand how working will affect your Social Security benefits?
What the Research Says: Social Security benefits are based on how much you earned during your working career and the age when you start claiming benefits. Social Security benefits may decrease and be taxed if you work while you claim benefits.

Many people continue to work beyond retirement age, either by choice or out of necessity. But if you are receiving Social Security benefits, you need to be aware of how working can affect your benefit payments. Earning income above Social Security thresholds can cause a reduction in benefits and mean your benefits will be taxed. Whether it makes sense to work and collect Social Security at the same time is a complicated assessment that depends on how much you earn and when you begin taking Social Security benefits.

If you work and are at full retirement age or older, you can earn as much as you want, and your benefits will not be reduced. However, individuals may begin taking Social Security retirement benefits early beginning at age 62. If you are younger than full retirement age, there is a limit to how much you can earn and still receive full benefits. For 2023, the maximum amount of earnings subject to the Social Security tax (taxable maximum) will increase to $160,200.

The earnings limit for workers who are younger than the "full" retirement age will increase from $19,560 to $21,240. (We deduct $1 from benefits for each $2 earned over $21,240.) The earnings limit for people reaching their "full" retirement age in 2023 will increase from $51,960 to $56,520. (We deduct $1 from benefits for each $3 earned over $56,520 until the month the worker turns "full" retirement age.) There is no limit on earnings for workers who are "full" retirement age or older for the entire year.

Another way that working can affect Social Security is with regard to taxes. If your combined income (Social Security calculates "combined income" by adding one-half of your Social Security benefits to your other income) is between $25,000 and $34,000 (or $32,000 and $44,000, if filing jointly), you may have to pay taxes on 50% of your benefits. If your income is more than $34,000 (or $44,000 if filing jointly), then you may have to pay taxes on up to 85% of your benefits.

Social Security and Supplemental Security Income (SSI) benefits for approximately 70 million Americans will increase to 8.7 percent in 2023. The 8.7 percent cost-of-living adjustment (COLA) will begin with benefits payable to more than 70 million Social Security beneficiaries in January 2023. It's highly recommended you speak to a retirement planner (vs. just relying on a Social Security calculator) who is skilled in the impacts of working on your Social Security benefits.

Below you will find a breakdown of benefit payments before and after the updated 8.7 percent COLA adjustment.

Estimated Average Monthly Social Security Benefits Payable in January 2023		
	Before 8.7% COLA	After 8.7% COLA
All Retired Workers	$1,681	$1,827
Aged Couple, Both Receiving Benefits	$2,734	$2,972
Widowed Mother and Two Children	$3,238	$3,520
Aged Widow(er) Alone	$1,567	$1,704
Disabled Worker, Spouse and One or More Children	$2,407	$2,616
All Disabled Workers	$1,364	$1,483

Question 29: Do you understand how provisional income and taxes impact your Social Security benefits?

What the Research Says: Provisional income is a measure used by the IRS to determine whether recipients of Social Security are required to pay taxes on their benefits. Provisional income is calculated by adding up a recipient's gross income, tax-free interest, and 50% of their Social Security benefits.

These three steps calculate provisional income:
1. Start with your gross income, which is the total amount of money you make not including your Social Security benefits. You can find this amount on your tax return.
2. Add any tax-free interest you received, such as interest from a municipal bond, which is always tax-exempt at the federal level.
3. Calculate 50% of your Social Security benefit and add that amount to your previous total.

For example, let's say your gross income is $20,000 and you earned $2,000 in municipal bond interest. Add those amounts together to arrive at $22,000. Now let's assume you receive $24,000 in Social Security benefits. Divide that in half to arrive at $12,000. Add $22,000 and $12,000, and your provisional income for tax purposes is $34,000.

How does Provisional Income Affect Taxation?

Your provisional income and your tax filing status decide whether, and how much, your Social Security benefits are taxed per the chart below:

Tax Filing Status	Provisional Income	Social Security Taxation
Single or head of household	Less than $25,000	0%
	$25,000–$34,000	Up to 50%
	More than $34,000	Up to 85%
Joint filers	Less than $32,000	0%
	$32,000–$44,000	Up to 50%
	More than $44,000	Up to 85%

It's highly recommended that you speak to a retirement planner who understands provisional income and the impact of taxes.

Question 30: Do you understand the issues with the solvency of the Social Security system and how it could impact you in retirement?
What the Research Says: According to the Social Security Administration, around 2034 they will have funds to pay for only approximately 75% of promised benefits. The main issue is that in 1945 there were 49 workers paying into the system for every one worker claiming their benefits. Today, there are 2.8 workers for every one worker claiming their benefits! This has created a tremendous drain on the system.

Since most people count Social Security for one-third of their retirement income, it's prudent to consider how you will cover this potential gap between what you would get today vs. a reduced amount by 2034.

Question 31: Do you understand the need to incorporate Social Security into an overall income projection analysis?
What the Research Says: As stated earlier, getting your Social Security filing strategy and timing right requires more than a simple, isolated calculation. It's critical to get a retirement income projection analysis done that incorporates Social Security (which is only 33% of your income picture) with your other savings and assets to make the best, most informed decision.

Home Equity

Question 32: Do you understand how a reverse mortgage could provide a guaranteed income buffer in retirement?

What the Research Says: According to Shelley Giordano, chair of the Funding Longevity Task Force and author of the book *What's the Deal with Reverse Mortgages?*, "A reverse mortgage can be used as a 'buffer asset' when a borrower utilizes a Home Equity Conversion Mortgage (HECM) early in retirement, rather than delaying acquisition until the borrower's portfolio has been depleted. By obtaining a HECM line of credit, the borrower can 'buffer' their investments during years when their portfolio experiences negative returns. The idea is to draw upon the HECM credit line in these circumstances instead of selling off certain investments, such as stocks, in efforts to weather market volatility."[31]

"Don Graves calls reverse mortgage loans the 'Swiss army knife of retirement income planning.' Graves, an adjunct professor of retirement income at the American College of Financial Services in Philadelphia, says the loan can be used strategically to address a range of retirement situations. 'Unexpected illness or inadequate savings are just two of the times a reverse mortgage loan can be a true lifesaver—or retirement-saver. But other situations can also benefit from a reverse mortgage loan.' "[32]

1. When a home represents the bulk of a homeowner's portfolio, a reverse mortgage loan is a way to create more money. Additionally, the loan can prevent the IRA or 401(k) from becoming a depleting asset that the retiree is forced to draw on more quickly.
2. Opening a line of credit through a HECM, gives you a way to tap into home equity to pay for things like "aging in place." This would allow you to leave your 401(k) untouched so it can be used as intended—for life in retirement.
3. The need for cash sometimes keeps people in their 70s in the workplace. For people who are house rich and cash poor, a HECM could provide extra money each month as it eases the burden of paying the mortgage on a home. The necessity of working is eliminated, and older homeowners can remain in their homes.
4. When home equity is the biggest asset, a HECM can be used to meet unanticipated expenses. For example, a widow or one spouse in a couple is losing mobility and needs in-home care but isn't sick enough to need an assisted living facility or a nursing home. Medicare does not entirely cover the costs of partial in-home care and assorted other out-of-pocket costs. People with meager retirement savings but with home equity can use the house to create cash flow. The homeowner can tap into a line of credit, either taking the payments as a lump sum or in monthly payments, like an annuity stream.

---

[31] Shelley Giordano, *What's the Deal with Reverse Mortgages?* (People Tested, 2015).
[32] Jill Cornfield, "7 Times a Reverse Mortgage Loan Can Save Your Retirement," *Bankrate*, https://www.bankrate.com/finance/mortgages/reverse-mortgage-can-save-retirement-1.aspx.

5. A HECM can be used as a way of hedging on market conditions. When the markets are doing well and they're getting good returns (on a retirement account), they can use their gains to pay for their retirement. When the market is not doing well, they can use the proceeds from the HECM. At the same time, someone can stay in their home longer, they also have more freedom not to draw on retirement funds in a down market.
6. You can use a HECM to purchase a new home.
7. You can use a HECM to help pay for your kids or grandkids to go to college. Or you can pay for health insurance during your early retirement years until Medicare kicks in when you turn 65. Or perhaps you will use it to pay Medicare Part B and Part D costs.

Dr. Wade Pfau, retirement researcher and author of *How to use Reverse Mortgages to Secure Your Retirement* provides some additional research-based insight on the use of home equity in retirement.

"Though reverse mortgages have long held a bad reputation, research and public policy in recent years are shedding new light on their potential uses in retirement. The vast majority of reverse mortgages in the United States are Home Equity Conversion Mortgage (HECM – commonly pronounced "heck-um") reverse mortgages, which are regulated and insured through the federal government by the Department of Housing and Urban Development (HUD) and the Federal Housing Authority (FHA).

Especially since 2013, the federal government has been refining regulations for its HECM program in order to improve the sustainability of the underlying mortgage insurance fund, to better protect eligible non-borrowing spouses, and ensure borrowers have sufficient financial resources to meet their homeowner obligations.

Financial planning research has shown that coordinated use of a reverse mortgage starting earlier in retirement outperforms waiting to open a reverse mortgage as a last resort option once all else has failed. Reverse mortgages have transitioned from the last resort to a retirement income tool that can be incorporated as part of an overall efficient retirement income plan. Two benefits give opening a reverse mortgage earlier in retirement the potential to improve retirement outcomes, even after accounting for loan costs.

First, coordinating retirement spending from a reverse mortgage reduces strain on the investment portfolio, which helps manage the risk of having to sell assets at a loss after market downturns. Reverse mortgages can help sidestep this risk by providing an alternative source of retirement spending after market declines, creating more opportunities for the portfolio to recover.

The second potential benefit of opening the reverse mortgage early—especially when interest rates are low—is that the principal limit (the overall eligible amount consisting of any loan balance and remaining line of credit) that you can borrow from will continue to grow throughout retirement."[33]

A retirement planner well-versed in Home Equity Conversion Mortgages can help you determine if using your home equity is a prudent strategy given all your other savings and assets.

Question 33: Do you understand how a reverse mortgage could provide tax-free income in retirement?
What the Research Says: As far as taxes go, there are pros and cons to reverse mortgages. On the plus side, reverse mortgages are considered loan advances to you, not income you earned. Thus, the payments you receive are not taxable. Moreover, they usually don't affect your Social Security or Medicare benefits.

However, all the interest that accrues on your reverse mortgage is not deductible by you until you actually pay it, which is usually when you pay off the loan in full. Moreover, your mortgage interest deduction is usually subject to the same limits as other home equity loans—that is, you can deduct the interest on no more than a loan of $100,000.

Question 34: Do you understand the details of how a reverse mortgage works and the common misconceptions?
What the Research Says: A Home Equity Conversion Mortgage (HECM), also known as a government-insured reverse mortgage loan, is a great tool to help you use the equity from your home and convert a portion of it into cash. Thousands of senior homeowners have taken advantage of this beneficial tool since its inception in 1961, and you may be able to as well. It's called a "reverse mortgage" because, instead of you paying the lender, the lender pays you. These payments can be a lump sum, a monthly advance, a line of credit, or a combination of those.

There are three basic types of reverse mortgages:
1. Single-purpose reverse mortgages, offered by some state and local government agencies and nonprofit organizations,
2. Federally insured reverse mortgages, known as Home Equity Conversion Mortgages (HECMs) and backed by the US Department of Housing and Urban Development (HUD), and

---

[33] Wade Pfau, "How to Use Reverse Mortgages to Secure Your Retirement," *Retirement Insights and Trends*, https://www.retirement-insight.com/use-reverse-mortgages-secure-retirement/.

3. Proprietary reverse mortgages are private loans that are backed by the companies that develop them.

When you take out a reverse mortgage, the title to your home remains with you and you continue to live in the home. You must continue to pay for repairs, property insurance, and taxes. When you move out, sell the home, or die (or the last surviving borrower dies), you or your estate will need to repay the loan. The loan balance will include the amount paid to you in cash, plus the interest and fees added to the loan balance each month. This means your total debt increases as the loan funds are paid to you and interest on the loan accrues. Usually, when the loan becomes due, you or your heirs will have to sell the home and use the proceeds to pay it off. You or your heirs can keep any money left over. If you or your heirs want to retain ownership of the home, you usually must repay the loan in full—even if the loan balance is greater than the value of the home.

Question 35: Do you understand the requirements to qualify for a reverse mortgage?
What the Research Says: Eligibility for reverse mortgages depends upon three requirements: 1. General requirements (age, homeownership, and others), 2. Home qualifications (HUD and FHA rules), and 3. Financial Qualifications (homeowner income and debt).

General Requirements:
- You must be at least 62 years or older (in some states you can apply at 60)—Since reverse mortgages were designed to help seniors age in their homes, this loan is available only to individuals of retirement age.
- You must own your home—Your name must be on the title of the home. You must also either own your home outright or have a low enough remaining mortgage balance for the reverse mortgage loan to pay it off.
- Your home must be your primary residence—Because this loan was meant to help seniors stay at home, borrowers must live in the home and cannot live elsewhere for more than 12 consecutive months.
- You must complete a counseling session with a HUD-approved counseling agency—The US Department of Housing and Urban Development (HUD) provides a list of third-party agencies for you to choose from for this counseling. The purpose of this requirement is so you are aware of all your options, and you can evenly weigh the pros and cons of each.

Home Qualifications:
- Your home must be a single-family home or a 4-unit maximum multiple-family home with one unit occupied by you—According to HUD, the most common type of property eligible for a reverse mortgage is a single-family home. If your property is a multiple-family home, then one of the units must be your primary residence.

- Your home can be a manufactured home if it meets FHA requirements—You can check the Federal Housing Administration's (FHA) website for these requirements.
- Your home can be a condominium if it is HUD-approved—More information about HUD-approved condos can be found on their website or through your reverse mortgage lender.

There are certain kinds of homes that simply do not qualify for a HECM loan. Vacation homes or secondary homes are not approved under reverse mortgage qualifications because they aren't considered the homeowner's primary residence. Also, if your home is on income-producing land such as a farm, then it is not eligible either.

Financial Qualifications:
- You must be financially able to pay your property taxes, insurance, home maintenance, and any applicable Home Owner's Association (HOA) fees—One of the most important things to remember about reverse mortgages is that you are still responsible for paying your property taxes, home insurance, and any home fees, like HOA fees, for the life of the loan. The benefits of reverse mortgages apply only if you comply with all loan terms; otherwise, you may be at risk of defaulting on the loan.
- You cannot be delinquent on any federal debt—These reverse mortgage qualifications and requirements may seem daunting, but don't let that prevent you from applying. A licensed professional can walk you through the whole process and let you know if there are other location-specific, property-specific, or borrower-specific requirements that you should be aware of. Many homeowners have found that once they satisfy the requirements for reverse mortgages, the benefits of this unique loan helped them achieve a better quality of life.[34]

Savings & Investments in Retirement

Question 36: Do you understand the role that your savings and investments will play in filling your gap between guaranteed income sources and expenses?

What the Research Says: For most of us, personal savings and investments will make up the bulk of our retirement income. When you retire, you'll be making decisions about what to do with the assets you currently hold...should you sell them, consolidate them, or move them around? You'll also need to determine whether you can generate enough income from them to fill your gap.

You might save for retirement using tax-advantaged vehicles such as 401(k)s and other employer-sponsored retirement plans, as well as IRAs. These savings vehicles may include a variety of investments including stocks, bonds, cash alternatives, mutual funds, and exchange-

---

[34] Mia Taylor, "What are the requirements for a reverse mortgage?" Bankrate, https://www.bankrate.com/mortgages/what-are-the-requirements-for-reverse-mortgages/.

traded funds (ETFs). Annuities can also be purchased to provide supplementary retirement income. You may also invest in taxable vehicles, typically securities purchased through brokerage accounts outside of retirement plans.

The return and principal value of stocks, mutual funds, ETFs, and bonds fluctuate with market conditions. Shares, when sold, may be worth more or less than their original cost. Supply and demand for ETF shares may cause them to trade at a premium or a discount relative to the value of the underlying shares. The FDIC insures CDs and bank savings accounts, which generally provide a fixed rate of return, up to $250,000 per depositor, per insured institution.

Note: Mutual funds, ETFs, and variable annuities are sold by prospectus. Consider the investment objectives, risks, charges, and expenses carefully before investing. The prospectus, which contains this and other information about the fund or the variable annuity contract and the underlying investment options, can be obtained from your financial professional. Be sure to read the prospectus carefully before deciding whether to invest.

Withdrawals from traditional IRAs, employer-sponsored retirement plans and annuities prior to age 59½ may be subject to a 10% federal income tax penalty. Distributions are taxed as ordinary income (with annuities, only earnings are taxed).

If you cannot generate enough of a "retirement paycheck" from your current savings and investments, you can make some sacrifices on expenses (such as not buying that latte every morning or giving up the gym membership you never use) and start socking away more into your savings and investments as one important option. As you'll see in the chart below, let's say you're 15 years from retirement and feeling behind, you could aim your sights on saving $15,000 a year, which will get you $439,864 more in your nest egg (assuming an 8% return rate)!

It's important to understand that Multi-Discipline Retirement Strategies (MDRS) can make what you have saved more efficient. These retirement-optimized strategies are not known to many financial advisors but are the unique purview of retirement planners. They include income distribution, portfolio allocation and management, Social Security timing, use of home equity, and tax minimization, along with creative long-term care funding. Their combination can potentially put you in a much stronger position with your portfolio, without adding a single cent to it. Before you get too stressed about what you have, have a retirement projection completed that includes the impact of MDRS on your portfolio. You might be surprised at the outcome.

Savings & Growth Over Time (the value of compound interest is demonstrated here)

Growing at 8% for	$10,000 Invested Annually	$15,000 Invested Annually	$20,000 Invested Annually
5 years	$63,359	$95,039	$126,719
10 years	$156,455	$234,682	$312,910
15 years	$293,243	$439,864	$586,486
20 years	$494,229	$741,344	$988,458
25 years	$789,544	$1.2 million	$1.6 million
30 years	$1.2 million	$1.8 million	$2.4 million

Question 37: Do you understand how your investment strategy will need to change in retirement so you don't run out of money later in life?

What the Research Says: Asset allocation or asset diversification is an investment strategy that attempts to balance risk and reward by providing an efficient blend of assets based on a person's investing goals, risk tolerance, and time horizon. The three main asset classes are usually stocks, bonds, and cash, each performing differently over time.

A relatively new fourth asset class called Fixed Index Annuities (FIAs) has emerged to address the need for retirees to have a more secure income source in retirement. The goal in retirement is to properly allocate the assets in your portfolio so that the portfolio survives as long as you do. The strategy deployed must balance the trade-off between growth and safety, and this balance changes the closer you get to retirement.

The traditional 60/40 stock/bond portfolio does not work for most retirees, as it represents too much risk on the stock side and too much allocation to bonds since bonds are currently at historic lows. There are other investment vehicles that can provide the safety of bonds but with much better growth. These include the asset class of Fixed Index Annuities and Structured Investments in a balanced combination.

The new, balanced portfolio that's recommended for today's retirees is what is referred to as the Hybrid Income Portfolio™ (HIP). The HIP typically reduces the allocation of stock to 40% focused on globally diversified stocks. This is to combat volatility risk. Thirty percent is allocated to principal-protected Fixed Indexed Annuities, which offer guarded growth with downside protection, and another 30% to Structured Investments.

Leading retirement research supports the value of FIAs in a retirement portfolio. In a report entitled, *"Fixed Indexed Annuities: Consider the Alternative,"* by Roger G. Ibbotson, Ph.D., Professor Emeritus of Finance, Yale School of Management (January 2018), the following conclusions were reached:

- A Fixed Indexed Annuity ("FIA") is a tax-deferred retirement savings vehicle that eliminates downside risk while allowing for the opportunity to participate in upside market returns.
- FIAs using a large-cap equity index outperformed long term bonds with similar risk characteristics and better downside protection over the period 1927-2016.[35]

In another research report, *Real-World Index Annuity Returns* by Geoffrey VanderPal, D.B.A, CFP®, CLU, CFS, RFC®; Jack Marrion; and David F. Babbel, Ph.D., Wharton School of Economics, UPenn, the following was concluded about the use of FIAs in a retirement portfolio:

- The returns of real-world fixed index annuities analyzed in this paper outperformed the S&P 500 Index over 67% of the time.
- The FIA's study outperformed a 50/50 mix of one-year Treasury bills and the S&P 500 Index 79% of the time.[36]

The proper investment strategy of a Hybrid Income Portfolio will also include tax-efficient withdrawals for tapping into your assets when needed. A retirement planner is skilled in creating retirement-optimized portfolios that provide the proper balance, whereas a traditional investment advisor might not fully understand the nuances, risks, and strategies unique to retirement. The asset allocation that's right for you depends on a variety of factors: your investment objectives, risk tolerance, time frame to retirement, safe withdrawal rate, net worth, sources of income, debt, health, and tolerance for loss. Note: There is no guarantee that working with a financial professional will improve investment results.

However, the right retirement planner will create a savings and investment strategy that protects against major losses and the risks mentioned earlier, while continuing your growth objectives.

---

[35] Ibbotson, Roger G. "Fixed Indexed Annuities: Consider the Alternative." Zebra Capital Management, January 2018.

[36] VanderPal, Geoffrey, Jack Marrion, and David F. Babbel. "Real World Index Annuity Returns." The Journal of Financial Planning. Accessed November 11, 2019, https://www.onefpa.org/journal/Pages/RealWorld%20Index%20Annuity%20Returns.aspx.

Question 38: Do you understand what percentage of conservative vs. aggressive components your portfolio should be, based on your age and risk tolerance?

What the Research Says: Many people have varying comfort levels with risk. A risk questionnaire can help you determine your risk tolerance. Financial advisors and retirement planners use the results as one component to building a portfolio you're comfortable with, suggesting allocations to conservative and aggressive components. Here's a sample of some questions you may be asked:

In general, how would your best friend describe you as a risk-taker?

    a. A real gambler. b. Willing to take risks after completing adequate research. c. Cautious. d. A real risk avoider.

You are on a TV game show and can choose one of the following. Which would you take?

    a. A cash prize of $1,000. b. A 50% chance of winning $5,000. c. A 25% chance at winning $10,000. d. A 5% chance at winning $100,000.

You can use the following questionnaire with a retirement planner to determine where you fall on the risk tolerance spectrum. You can use a scale of 1–5 with 1 being disagreed and 5 strongly agree.

    __I am more concerned about protecting my assets than about growth.
    __I prefer the ease of mutual funds to the uncertainty of trying to pick winning stocks.
    __Professional advisors and mutual funds may achieve higher growth than I can.
    __I'm comfortable with investments that promise slow, long-term appreciation & growth.
    __ I don't brood over bad investment decisions I have made.
    __ I feel comfortable with aggressive growth investments.
    __ I do not like surprises.
    __ I am optimistic about my financial future.
    __ My immediate concern is for income rather than growth opportunities.
    __ I am a risk-taker.
    __ I make investment decisions comfortably and quickly.
    __ I like predictability and routine in my daily life.
    __ I usually pick the tried and true, the slow, safe but sure investments.
    __ I need to focus my investment efforts on reserve funds and insurance rather than growth.
    __ I prefer predictable, steady returns on my investments, even if the return is low.

Question: 39: Do you understand the concept of the safe withdrawal rate and how it impacts the longevity of your portfolio?

What the Research Says: Determining how much income you can withdraw from your assets is the logical next step in your income planning process. People often underestimate the importance of determining their safe withdrawal rate, which is the rate at which you can "safely" pull money out of your portfolio while keeping it intact for your lifetime.

What Is the Safe Withdrawal Rate (SWR) Method?

"The safe withdrawal rate (SWR) method is one way that retirees can determine how much money they can withdraw from their accounts each year without running out of money before reaching the end of their lives. The safe withdrawal rate method is a conservative approach that tries to balance having enough money to live comfortably with not depleting retirement savings prematurely. It is based largely on the portfolio's value at the beginning of retirement."[37]

The Safe Withdrawal Rate Method Explained

Figuring out how to use your retirement savings isn't easy because there are so many unknowns, including how the market will perform, how high inflation will be, and whether you will develop additional expenses (such as medical), and what your life expectancy is. The longer you expect to live, the faster you could draw down your savings; in addition, the worse the market performs, the more likely you are to run out of money.

The safe withdrawal rate method tries to prevent these worst-case scenarios from happening by instructing retirees to take out only a small percentage of their portfolio each year, traditionally 3% to 4%. Financial experts recommended safe withdrawal rates have changed over the years as experience has illustrated what really works and what doesn't work and why.

Knowing what safe withdrawal rate you'd like to use in retirement also informs how much you need to save during your working years. If you want an SWR of 4%, you need to save more than if you want an SWR of 3%. The rate you choose affects how aggressively you need to save and how long you need to work.

Limitations of the Safe Withdrawal Rate Method

A shortcoming of the safe withdrawal rate method is that depending on when you retire, the economic conditions can be very different from what initial retirement models assume. A 4% withdrawal rate may be safe for one retiree yet cause another to run out of money prematurely, depending on factors such as asset allocation and investment returns during retirement.

In addition, retirees don't want to be overly conservative in choosing a safe withdrawal rate because that will mean living on less than necessary during retirement when it would have been possible to enjoy a higher standard of living. Ideally, though this is rarely possible because

---

[37] Adam Hayes, "Safe Withdrawal Rate (SWR) Method," *Investopedia*, January 28, 2019, https://www.investopedia.com/terms/s/safe-withdrawal-rate-swr-method.asp.

of all the unpredictable factors involved, a safe withdrawal rate means having exactly $0 when you die, or if you want to leave an inheritance, having exactly the sum you want to bequeath.

We like to consider it your Safe, Tax-Efficient Withdrawal Strategy™ (STEWS for short). The goal of your plan is to make your income (or distribution strategy) in retirement as efficient and sustainable as possible. STEWS is designed to do just that.

What is the right amount typically? The conventional wisdom of William Bengen's "4% safe withdrawal rule" established in 1994 is being strongly refuted in today's low-interest-rate environment. Bengen based his findings on historical data dating back to 1926 with a portfolio that was invested 50% in S&P 500 stocks and 50% in intermediate-term government bonds. He suggested that a retiree would be safe pulling 4% out of a portfolio over the course of a 30-year retirement. For example, if you retire with $1,000,000, you could afford to take a withdrawal of $40,000 (4%) in the first year of retirement, increase it for inflation each year, and sustain that income stream for 30 years. The safe withdrawal rate dispels the common misunderstanding that if the average return on the portfolio was 7%–8% then that amount can be withdrawn each year. Because of the ups and downs of the market, the sustainable withdrawal amount is much less than the average return on the portfolio.

However, a 2013 research report conducted by Morningstar Investment Management entitled, *Low Bond Yields and Safe Portfolio Withdrawal Rates* belies the 4% rule and adjusts the safe withdrawal rate down to 2.4% when investing in a 60% stock/40% bond portfolio with a 30-year retirement time horizon. According to the Morningstar report, "Yields on government bonds are well below historical averages. These low yields will have a significant impact on retirees who tend to invest heavily in bonds. This is because portfolio returns in the earliest years of retirement have a larger impact on the likelihood that a retirement income strategy will succeed than returns later in retirement; this is known as sequence risk. We find a significant reduction in 'safe' initial withdrawal rates, with a 4% initial real withdrawal rate having approximately a 50% probability of success over a 30-year period."[38]

This new data begs the question, "How can one live on a 2.4% withdrawal rate?" As stated simply, it's not likely. Enter the Multi-Discipline Strategies (MDRS) that we have discussed previously. They work together to increase the amount of money you can safely withdraw getting us not only back up to Bengen's 4% rule but even higher to 6% or more! Alternatively, they can help you have monies left over to leave to your heirs.

Once we've addressed how much, we need to address how? There are many withdrawal methods for how you can withdraw your money. They include:

---

[38]David Blanchett, Michael Finke, and Wade D. Pfau, "Low Bond Yields and Safe Portfolio Withdrawal Rates." *Morningstar Investment*, January 21, 2013, https://news.morningstar.com/pdfs/blanchett_lowbondyield_1301291.pdf.

Systematic withdrawals: Choosing a fixed dollar amount on a regular schedule, a specific percentage of the account value on a regular schedule, or the total value of the account in equal distributions over a specified period of time.

Endowment method: The endowment method begins with an initial withdrawal of a fixed percentage, typically 3% to 5%. In subsequent years, the same fixed percentage is applied to the remaining assets. So, the actual withdrawal amount may go up or down depending on previous withdrawals and market performance. A modified version of the endowment method applies a ceiling and/or a floor to the change in your withdrawal amount.

Life expectancy method: With this method, you withdraw an increasing percentage of your portfolio each year based on your life expectancy. Put another way, each year you would divide your total portfolio by your life expectancy.

Three-tiered strategy: This evens out the sequence of return risks. For Tier 1, you estimate how much you might need to live on over the next 2–3 years and invest that money in conservative assets such as cash and cash alternatives. For money you would need from 3 to 10 years (Tier 2), you would invest primarily in fixed-income vehicles that offer the potential for moderate returns, but this also comes with some price volatility. You might also consider some stocks for this tier. For monies not needed for a decade or more, you would keep Tier 3 assets invested in more aggressive investments to provide future growth potential. Throughout your retirement, you would periodically shift assets from the long- and medium-term tiers downward to provide for your short-term needs.

A retirement planner is best suited to help you sort through your safe withdrawal rate and guard against Portfolio Overdraft while helping you implement strategies to maximize the amount you can safely withdraw to cover your retirement needs. He/she will also be able to help you determine the withdrawal method that's best for your particular needs.

Question 40: Do you understand how sequence-of-return risk and withdrawing too much when your portfolio has lost value can have a lasting negative effect on your retirement?
What the Research Says: Sequence risk is the danger that the timing of withdrawals from a retirement account will damage the investor's overall return. Its impact is felt when you are adding or withdrawing money from your investments.

During your retirement years, if a high proportion of negative returns occur in the beginning years of your retirement, it will have a lasting negative effect and reduce the amount of income you can withdraw over your lifetime. When you're retired, you will most likely need to sell investments periodically to create your retirement paycheck. If the negative returns occur first, you'll end up selling some investments, thereby reducing the amount that could be impacted by later-occurring positive returns. Protecting against sequence risk means anticipating a worst-case scenario. Don't assume that a bull market will reign throughout your golden years. Timing is everything!

To help mitigate the sequence of return risk:
- Consider working as late as you can to contribute more to your retirement account, particularly in your peak earning years.
- Keep saving and investing even after you retire. If you're past age 70 1/2, you can't use a traditional IRA, but you can contribute to a Roth IRA or, for that matter, open a personal investment account.
- Diversify your portfolio and consider fixed index annuities as a hedge against sequence risk and volatility.

It's critical that your income projection and portfolio are "stress-tested" against all market environments (negative, average, and positive). You'll want to make sure that you can survive in a negative market. If you cannot, you'll need to adjust your plan. This is the basis of a strong plan…be prepared for the worst and hope for the best.

Question 41: Do you understand the value of running multiple portfolio scenarios with different growth and inflation assumptions, while also determining your safe withdrawal rate?
What the Research Says: Your income projection must incorporate inflation risks and various portfolio allocations. A number of Monte Carlo simulations will give you scenarios to make the best possible decisions while showing you your optimal safe withdrawal amount.

Question 42: Do you understand the amount of your savings held in long-term bonds and bond mutual funds, and the impact changes in interest rates may have on them?
What the Research Says: Like all types of investments, bonds are subject to risks.
For example, if you sell a bond before the end of its term, also known as its maturity date, it may be worth more or less than what you originally paid for it. That's due to interest rate risk. Bond prices are sensitive to changes in interest rates. As interest rates rise, the value of existing bonds typically falls. This happens because in a higher interest rate environment, newly issued bonds offer higher interest payments, or yields, than what existing bonds are providing. Therefore, existing bonds are worth less on the financial markets than new bonds that offer higher rates.

On the other hand, if interest rates fall, the value of existing bonds will rise. Because newer bonds will be issued at lower rates, your higher-interest bond may command a premium if you sell it before it reaches maturity. The value of a bond may also suffer if the issuer's credit rating declines while the bond is outstanding.

Question 43: Do you understand how the current state of bonds affects the traditional 60/40 portfolio and why they aren't the best "safe money" solution currently?
What the Research Says: In the current interest rate market, bond values are at all-time lows. Therefore, you'll want to consider other safe money alternatives such as Fixed Index annuities (FIAs) in your portfolio.

A research report from Investment advisory firm Hedgewise, *Most Bond Investors Fear Rising Interest Rates? Insights from 1958 to 1982,* examined the effect rising interest rates had on 20-year treasury bond returns from 1958 through 1982. They concluded in their report, "The overall return for this 23-year period was approximately 48% cumulative return or about 1.7% average annualized return. More importantly, the results were far from consistent, as bonds both rallied and fell for different stretches throughout."[39]

Let's take a quick look at FIA vs. high-quality government bonds and their relationship to interest rate movements:
- Bonds have an inverse relationship to interest rates.
    - As interest rates rise, bonds generally lose value.
    - As interest rates decline, bonds generally gain capital appreciation potential.

- FIAs typically have a positive relationship to interest rate movements.
    - As interest rates rise, FIA renewal rates generally increase.
    - As interest rates decline, FIA renewal rates will generally decline.

In summary, a 5-year treasury yield is 1.736% and the 10-year yield is 1.921, according to CNBC.com as of 11/11/19.[40] If interest rates hold at these levels or increase over the foreseeable future, FIAs will offer value over high-quality bonds. If interest rates decline over the foreseeable future, bonds will pick up capital appreciation and will be a viable "safe money" alternative. In this low-interest rate environment, with the high probability of increasing rates, FIAs are a viable "safe money" alternative to bonds. Investors expecting bond funds to perform as well in the next ten years as they have in the last ten will be disappointed. As previously discussed, bonds can play an important role in retirement portfolios, reducing volatility, and increasing the predictability of returns. However, the stellar performance of bonds from 1982

---

[39] "Must Bond Investors Fear Rising Interest Rates? Insights from 1958 to 1982." *Hedgewise*, December 3, 2014, https://seekingalpha.com/article/2728105-must-bond-investors-fear-rising-interest-rates-insights-from-1958-to-1982.
[40] Sam Meredith, Yun Li, "Treasury Yields Fall Slightly as US-China Trade Remains in Focus."

through 2017 (decreasing interest rate environment) will not be repeated anytime soon. In fact, there is even the risk of *negative* returns.

Question 44: Do you understand the differences among types of annuities and in what part of your safe money plan they could be included?

What the Research Says: Annuities, specifically Fixed Index Annuities (FIAs) are a new asset class being used in lieu of bonds in a retiree's portfolio. They are *not* a replacement for stocks. They provide a safe, guaranteed alternative to bonds. FIAs are a hybrid annuity – they are an insurance product, but they are tied to a stock market index. Therefore, you can have the safety of an insurance product along with the moderate growth of a securities product. There are many other types of annuities. It's important to have a basic understanding of each since there are over-zealous insurance agents out there willing to sell you an annuity. As a new asset class is brought into a retiree's portfolio, it's important that the advisor you work with understands how the combination of stock/bonds/annuities/structured investments works together to give you the best potential retirement outcome possible, while balancing the right risk/reward for your goals.

A recent research study commissioned by Nationwide Financial and completed by Morningstar Investment Management LLC compared a traditional 60/40 stock and bond portfolio to a portfolio consisting of stocks, bonds, and Fixed Index Annuities (FIAs). The study concluded that repositioning a traditional retirement portfolio consisting of 60% equities and 40% bonds to a portfolio consisting of 36% equities, 24% bonds, and 40% Fixed Index Annuities (FIAs) offers virtually the same return, but with a 40% reduction in potential portfolio risk and volatility...both of which are the number one objective for your portfolio as you head into retirement. The study used Nationwide's New Heights Fixed Index Annuity in combination with stock and bond indexes to compile the results.

There are two basic types of fixed annuities—immediate and deferred. Each type is used for distinctly different purposes.

Immediate annuities provide current income. Once you pay the premium, you will begin receiving a regular income, which is guaranteed by the issuing insurance company. That's what makes immediate annuities so appealing to people who are retiring and want to re-allocate their savings and investments for greater income.

Here are some of the advantages of immediate annuities:
- You start receiving income right away.
- You cannot outlive your retirement savings.
- You have a stable, locked-in income stream. Annuity funds are guaranteed by the assets of the company you buy them from.

- You don't have to take any further steps once you've purchased your annuity, and you don't need to monitor your investment.
- An immediate annuity can allow you to defer taxes until later in retirement. If you use a tax-deferred account to fund an annuity, then you'll only pay taxes as you receive the income, rather than all at once.
- The payments can be higher than the returns on other safe investments like certificates of deposit. However, keep in mind that some of your annuity payments consist of return of principal. Your total returns with an annuity are likely to be rather small compared with riskier investments.

Now let's consider the drawbacks:
- The benefit expires when you die. As you'll read shortly, you can buy annuities that are guaranteed for a certain period, but these come with lower payments.
- If you need access to your money (such as in an emergency), you won't have access to the principal you paid.
- Loss of purchasing power over time (unless you buy an inflation-protected annuity) will result in a lower initial monthly income.
- The fees associated with buying an annuity can be high.

Deferred annuities are designed for long-term accumulation. Typically, they're purchased during an individual's working years to allow the funds to grow. As their name implies, deferred annuities postpone the income you will receive to some future date. The premiums you pay earn interest. This doesn't mean you can't take out your money if you need it, but while the annuity is accumulating tax-deferred, you aren't receiving any income.

The earnings credited to a tax-deferred annuity are not taxed until they are withdrawn. When you do begin receiving payments from the annuity, the payments will reflect the added value from this tax-deferred accumulation.

Deferred annuities typically give you several options for getting your money, including lump-sum (you get your entire payment at once), systematic withdrawal (you periodically withdraw funds until your account is empty), and annuitization (you lock in a regular schedule of payments for a certain length of time). Check your annuity contract before you sign to see which options are available and to determine how your choice will affect how much money you get back. You'll need to wait until you're at least age 59½ to trigger payments of any sort, or you'll likely be hit with a 10% early withdrawal penalty by the IRS.

As long as you haven't annuitized your deferred annuity, you'll have access to the money you've contributed, and you can withdraw part of it or even cancel the contract—although you may have to pay surrender fees to do so. But once you do annuitize, you'll be locked into the payments set by your contract and will no longer be able to withdraw the money you've invested.

A retirement planner can help you decide which type of annuity is right for you.

Note: Generally, all annuities have contract limitations, fees, and sales charges, which may include mortality and expense charges, investment management fees, administrative fees, and charges for optional benefits. Surrender charges may be assessed during the early years of the contract if the annuity is surrendered. The guarantees of annuities are contingent on the financial strength and claims-paying ability of the issuing insurance company. The investment return and principal value of an investment option are not guaranteed. Variable annuity subaccounts fluctuate with changes in market conditions. When the annuity is surrendered, the principal may be worth more or less than the original amount invested.

Question 45: Do you understand how ETFs and structured investments and other income-producing financial vehicles could work in your retirement portfolio?

What the Research Says: Exchange-traded funds (ETFs) and structured investments are alternative viable investments many pre-retirees will want to consider for a portion of their portfolio. ETFs are low-cost with preferential tax treatment. Structured products offer investors the potential to earn returns tied to the performance of an index or basket of securities. Rates of return vary and are generally paid at maturity, along with the face amount of the investment, subject to the credit risk of the issuer.

Income-oriented mutual funds invest primarily in a variety of high-quality corporate bonds, lower-grade bonds, dividend-paying stocks, or a combination of these securities, depending on the fund's objectives. This can give you enhanced diversification, as well as the flexibility to customize your portfolio.

Some companies distribute a portion of profits to stockholders in the form of a dividend, these are called dividend-paying stocks. These stocks can also provide growth in your portfolio. Dividends are not guaranteed, and the amount paid to shareholders fluctuates as determined by the company. A retiree could use stock to generate a regular income by selling a set number of shares each month. Taxes would be due on any capital gains. Remember: return and principal value of stocks fluctuate with changes in market conditions (volatility). Shares, when sold, may be worth more or less than their original cost.

People who find themselves in higher tax brackets may be attracted to another option: tax-exempt investments. These include municipal bonds (or munis), treasuries, and tax-free money market funds. Munis are free of federal income tax and may be free of state and local income taxes for investors who live in the jurisdiction where the bond is issued. Treasuries are taxable at the federal level but are generally tax-exempt at the state level. Tax-free money market funds invest in a pool of short-term, tax-exempt municipal securities. The yield on a tax-exempt investment is typically lower than the yield on a similar taxable investment. A retirement planner can help you decide which type of tax-exempt investing is right for you.

Question 46: Do you understand the importance of and differences between strategic and tactical asset allocation?

What the Research Says: The goal of this planning platform is to help you be a better steward of your money and your retirement. Understanding strategic vs. tactical asset allocation approaches, along with their historical data, will help you toward this end.

In its simplest form, asset allocation explains how your money is divided into various financial assets such as stocks, bonds, and cash. The reason we rely on asset allocation is so that when one asset decreases in value, you'll have other assets that will keep your portfolio going strong. As stated previously, your asset allocation decision depends on your risk tolerance and time horizon. The younger you are, the more risk-tolerant you typically are and will therefore have a greater allocation to stocks, which may have you positioned up to 80% in stocks and 20% in safer options.

The traditional retirement allocation suggests investing 60% in stocks and 40% in bonds, but the "standard" retirement portfolio for a new economy suggests a Hybrid Income Portfolio™ of 30% global stocks, 30% structured investment products, and 40% Fixed Index Annuities offering a slight increase in return, but with at least a 50% reduction in portfolio risk. The split between stocks, SIPs, and FIAs can vary depending on an individual's goals and risk tolerance.

The difference between strategic and tactical asset allocations comes down to timing. Strategic allocations to various asset classes set the long-term target. To keep on track, investors rebalance back to the initial mix. Tactical allocation, on the other hand, is implemented based on current market conditions and is adjusted periodically. As an example, if an advisor senses a recession, a tactical allocation will entail selling stocks and increasing cash holdings or fixed investments (selling stock to buy bonds). This approach attempts to protect stock investments from a possible future loss in value.

With the pros and cons of both approaches, tactical tends to be more difficult to get right on a consistent basis. You'll need to have good luck accurately predicting the future and then taking the appropriate action at just the right moments. Stated another way, you need to be good at timing the market. The additional challenge is picking the right actively managed fund or manager. For most individuals, the tactical approach is riddled with risks including volatility, loss of capital, and other behavioral issues that come into play.

Question 47: Do you understand the critical need to regularly benchmark your portfolio to assess its relative value vs. just considering the absolute return?

What the Research Says: The most accurate gauge of assessing the value of each fund within your portfolio is to analyze performance relative to an industry benchmark. Many people simply look at their absolute returns without understanding how their funds did compare to a benchmark such as the S&P 500. The idea is that your funds should be performing at least at the benchmark level, but preferably above the benchmark.

Most investors understand their absolute returns, meaning they understand that their portfolio grew by a certain percentage on an annual basis. However, it's much more important to understand your relative returns, which means you're comparing your return relative to a proper investment industry benchmark.

As an example, if you invested in a large company US-based stock fund and you received a 9.27% net rate of return, that is your "absolute" return. Since this 9.27% is not compared to any applicable benchmark or index, there is no way to determine whether this rate of return was a good return, a bad return, or an average return.

If you invested in a large company US-based stock fund and received a 9.27% rate of return during a specific period and the average rate of return of all other large company US stock funds returned 10.96% during the same period, then your relative return vs. the average manager was –1.69%.

Most individual investors have no idea what their relative returns are vs. the appropriate benchmark. Benchmarking your portfolio versus the appropriate index is essential to prudent investment management. Relative returns are the most important factor when determining the effectiveness of any investment management style or strategy and must be compared to the appropriate style or index (net of overall fees or costs). This is also a good way to measure the performance of your advisor. He or she should be evaluating performance relative to a benchmark vs. just absolute return.

Question 48: Do you understand how the combination of low-cost passive index funds and ETFs with actively managed funds can potentially reduce fees and increase your returns?

What the Research Says: Index funds and exchange-traded funds typically use passive indexes and charge a fraction of the fees that most active money managers charge. They also have low turnover in their portfolios, keeping costs low. However, while less expensive, these funds won't outperform the index since they basically invest in the index. Meanwhile, actively managed funds are managed to outperform the indexes. It is critical to pick active managers with care, choosing those with low fees and positive results in both negative and positive markets, as well as those with low turnover (which is the percent of holdings that are bought and sold each year).

Recent research indicates that active managers outperform passive strategies in some asset classes, while passive strategies outperform in others. Historically, active strategies tend to perform better in down markets while passive strategies outperform in up markets. Morgan Stanley found that over the last 20 years, the top 25% of portfolio managers significantly outperformed their benchmarks in years when the market was down. Using low-cost passive index funds in combination with active managers can offer a lower cost and potentially a higher-performing portfolio.

Because there are thousands and thousands of funds, Exchange Traded Funds (ETFs), and individual portfolio managers for an investor to choose from, it is advisable that adequate research be used when selecting the proper asset allocation and investments for inclusion in the portfolio. As a result of these complexities, many people opt to work with an investment advisor or retirement planner. Here again, the informed investor will pay less in investment and advice fees.

Question 49: Do you understand the importance of a reserve fund and the minimum amount of emergency savings you should maintain throughout retirement?
What the Research Says: It's recommended that you have at least three times your annual income in an emergency fund. Some people feel more comfortable having more. The actual amount is an individual choice. However, too much in a banking product is not the best idea since returns are so low.

Question 50: Do you understand all the fees you are paying for your portfolio management?
What the Research Says: Fees can take a big bite out of your portfolio. It's important to ask your advisor for 100% transparency into the fees you will pay for services and products. If there's any hesitation, or if he or she has a hard time providing a straight answer, you may want to move on to another advisor. Hybrid Retirement Planners typically offer hybrid fee structures designed around what's best for your particular situation. Price is only an issue in the absence of value so make sure to understand all the services your advisor offers for the fee you are paying.
Here are some questions to consider:

1. Can you explain your fee structure?
2. Are you paid commissions on investments or other products you sell?
3. Aside from what I pay you, what other costs will I incur?
4. What are the services you provide for your fees?

A true retirement planner vs. an investment advisor will offer much more in the way of service, beyond just portfolio management. Keep in mind these differences in your comparisons and make sure you're not comparing apples to oranges.

Question 51: Do you understand the impact reduced fees could have on your portfolio?
What the Research Says: The easiest way to understand the impact of fees is through a case study.

In this scenario, the retiree has IRA Retirement Assets of $1,000,000.
The annual income generated (age 65–95) is $30,000/year (inflated at 3% per yr.).
The annual assumed rate of return is 6%.

Annual Fee	Total Retirement Income Generated Age 65–95	Total Portfolio Balance Age 95
1.00%	$ 1,691,948	$ 1,056,226
1.50%	$ 1,559,535	$ 705,813
2.00%	$ 1,442,797	$ 0

Which fee would you rather pay? It's important to understand how the investment industry works and how fees are assessed and paid. The type of financial product being used within your portfolio will determine the total fees that an investor will be paying to manage the account. A high-quality portfolio with low total fees gives you a better return potential.

401(k)/IRA Savings

Question 52: Do you understand how much you should contribute to your 401(k)/403b (also known as a defined contribution plan)?
What the Research Says: The most standard answer to this question, according to numerous studies, is at least 15% each year. If you start early on in your career and are consistent in your contributions, you will build a hefty account balance by the time retirement rolls around.

Here are the 2021 contribution limits for both 401(k)s and IRA/Roth IRAs. The government also allows catch-up contributions for people over 50.

401(k) Plan	IRA & Roth IRA
(Regular Contributions)	(Regular Contributions)
$22,500 + Catch-Up: $7,500	$6,500 + Catch-Up: $1,000
Total: $30,000	Total: $7,500

This means super-savers age 50-plus can sock away $37,500 in these tax-advantaged accounts for 2023. If your employer allows after-tax contributions or you're self-employed, you can save even more. The total employer-plus-employee limit is $66,000 .

Question 53: Do you understand how you should invest your retirement savings and stay on top of performance?
What the Research Says: Most plan participants have access to investment advice from the plan provider or a software program that helps form a basic recommendation based on factors such as age, gender, and risk tolerance. While you can certainly do your own research, you can also hire an outside advisor who can provide sound advice.

Once the investment decisions have been made, you'll want to stay the course and ride out any market volatility. You should also have your investment allocations checked at least once per year. All 401(k) plans let participants know how their plan is performing and if they're on track with their savings goals. Just remember, they don't always offer independent advice on how to allocate your savings.

A retirement planner can help you determine if your 401(k) is okay by doing an annual assessment and helping you make any adjustments in your investment options and to maximize your returns.

Question 54: Do you understand what's better? Traditional pre-tax 401(k) or a Roth 401(k) contributions?
What the Research Says: Roth 401(k) contributions are made after-tax, while traditional 401(k) contributions are made pre-tax. As a result, there isn't any immediate benefit to a Roth contribution, but the benefit in retirement could be a big one.

If a Roth 401(k) contribution account has been in existence for five years or more and if funds are withdrawn due to retirement, the entire account balance can be distributed tax-free. There's no way to know today if a traditional 401(k) or Roth 401(k) contribution is better since the answer depends on future tax rates. So, the most prudent guidance is to place both bets and split contributions between a traditional AND a Roth 401(k).

The split you employ is age dependent. Here's what the research says:

Age	**Percent Contribution**
20s	100% to Roth 401(k) for as long as possible

(It is highly likely tax rates will be higher in retirement years down the road...building tax-free savings is a really big benefit)

60s/70s	80–90% to Traditional 401(k)

(Most people in this age bracket have higher tax rates and fewer years to retirement. They benefit from immediate tax savings)

All ages in between	50% to Roth 401(k) and 50% to traditional 401(k)

A retirement planner can help make sure you have your traditional and Roth 401(k) strategies set-up properly, as well as your allocations.

Question 55. Do you understand how to tell if you have a well-defined contribution plan?
What the Research Says: Here are seven ways to tell if your employer offers a good plan.

1. Availability of low-cost (non-index fund) investment options
2. Prevalence of index funds
3. Availability of investment advice
4. Availability of projection tools
5. Performance tracking
6. Company's support of the plan
7. How well the provider helps you understand your plan and options

If you're not completely happy with your company's savings plan or your small employer doesn't offer one, consider these options.[41]

Consider an IRA
An IRA is the best option if your employer does not offer retirement benefits. This can be set up with a retirement planner. You and your planner can choose the type of investments that you want to make. You also have the option of choosing a traditional IRA or a Roth IRA. With a traditional IRA, your contributions grow tax-free, and you pay taxes when you take the money out in retirement.

With a Roth IRA, your contributions are not tax-deductible (i.e., they are made with after-tax dollars), but you are not taxed on the money and their earnings when you take it out for retirement. However, you are only eligible to contribute to a Roth IRA if you make less than $120,000 if you're single and $189,000 if you're married and file your taxes jointly.

While both Roth and traditional IRAs are great investment vehicles, generally a Roth IRA is a better choice (assuming you fall under the earning cap) if you expect to be in a higher tax bracket when you retire. A traditional IRA is a better choice if you expect to be in a lower tax bracket when you retire.

If this seems like too much for your own budget (the former breaks down to $500/month), don't get discouraged. You can work to increase this amount each year until you can contribute the maximum.

---

[41] Lorie Konish, "If your employer doesn't offer a 401(k), you can still save for retirement. Here's how," CNBC.com, October 24, 2018, https://www.cnbc.com/2018/10/24/how-you-can-save-for-retirement-even-if-your-employer-has-no-401k.html.

Self-Employment Options
If you are self-employed or an independent contractor, you have additional retirement options. You can enroll in a SEP IRA or a solo 401(k) plan. A SEP IRA is also a tax-advantaged retirement savings tool, in which your pre-tax money is invested tax-deferred until you take it out at retirement. A major benefit of a SEP IRA is the high contribution limit, which was $54,000 in 2017, not to exceed 25% of your income. Another retirement savings tool you may consider is a solo 401(k) plan.

Remember, it's a good idea to talk to your accountant or retirement planner about the best options for your retirement savings so that you can take advantage of as many tax breaks as possible while you are saving for retirement.

Consider Switching Jobs
When you first start working, you may be willing to go without some benefits to gain experience or because you really believe in a company. Some startups may not have retirement plans in the first few years but plan to offer them after that. If you are working at a smaller company or startup and have been there for a few years with no change in retirement benefits, you may want to consider switching jobs to a more established company to make the most out of your retirement savings and gain other valuable benefits.

Investing for Retirement Outside of Retirement Accounts
Just because you reach your maximum allowed contributions does not mean that you must stop contributing to retirement. You can save for retirement with traditional investments without it being in an official retirement account.

In fact, if you are planning on retiring early, you will want to have a good portion of your retirement benefits in separate accounts so that you can access the money without receiving an early withdrawal penalty. You are not allowed to take money out from either an IRA or a 401(k) until you are 59½ without a 10% penalty. But you may want to retire earlier than that if it's financially feasible for you to do so. If you have other investments, you can withdraw money from there until you reach age 59½ to avoid those penalties.

Take Advantage of Other Benefits
If you are working for a startup, they may offer other options, like buying stock options instead of a retirement account. This can allow you to benefit from the growth of the company in the first few years. This is a good option when managed correctly. You should make sure your portfolio is extremely diversified, especially since owning this type of stock is riskier, as a startup could fold unexpectedly. There are also rules about how soon you can sell your stock after purchasing, which vary by company, so this should not be your entire retirement plan.

Question 56. Do you understand the options for rolling over a 401(k) when separating from service?

What the Research Says: 25% of 401(k) participants 45 and older say they don't know what they'll do with their retirement account when they retire, according to a survey of 1,000 people with a 401(k) account conducted for Cerulli Associates, a research and consulting firm. Another 25% said they'll ask their financial advisor what to do, which is another way of saying they're not sure what to do.[42]

When you take a 401(k) from an old job, you have a few options on what to do with it. But for many people, a great choice is to convert it into an IRA. Rolling your 401(k) to an IRA offers some nice perks, including:
- A more diverse investment selection than a typical 401(k) plan,
- Cheaper investments (the cost comparison will depend on your employer's investment offerings), and
- Cheaper account fees. While some 401(k) plans pass account management fees along to the employees, many IRAs charge no account fees.

Leaving money in a 401(k) has some benefits, too, including the fact that your 401(k) is better protected from creditors. Also, generally, you can take a loan from a 401(k), which isn't possible with an IRA (though IRAs offer some loopholes for early withdrawals).

If you've decided a rollover IRA is right for you, here's how to make it happen. There's a right way to roll over your funds from a 401(k) and a wrong way. You don't want the 401(k) provider to cut a check in your name, and you don't want to cash out your balance. In both scenarios, you're at risk of owing up to a third of your balance to the IRS.

Take these four steps to rollover your funds without incurring any unpleasant tax surprises:
1. Decide on a Roth or a traditional IRA. If you roll into a Roth IRA, you'll owe taxes on the rolled amount. If you want to roll over your funds without incurring taxes, stick with a traditional IRA. (There's an exception: If you're rolling from a Roth 401(k), you won't incur taxes when you roll to a Roth IRA).
2. Open a rollover IRA account. Opening a rollover IRA account is easy and fast. Once you pick a provider, they'll ask for some information, including birthdate and Social Security number.
3. Ask your 401(k) plan for a "direct rollover." These two words are important: They mean that the 401(k) plan will cut a check directly to your new IRA account, not to you personally.
4. Choose your investments. Your 401(k) funds will enter the IRA as cash, so you'll need to invest the money. You can choose a provider who will pick your investments and

---

[42] Andrea Coombes, "What to Do with Your 401(k) When You Retire," *Nerdwallet*, https://www.nerdwallet.com/blog/investing/what-to-do-with-your-401k-when-you-retire/.

manage your money for you, or you can pick your investments and manage them yourself.

IRA rollovers are certainly a better option than cashing out, which is one of the most frivolous things you can do with a 401(k) account, other than not finding one in the first place. But moving money from a workplace retirement plan to an IRA when you switch jobs or retire may not be the best idea for you. When is a rollover the right choice? Sometimes plan sponsors don't do their jobs, of course, and it could be that your 401(k) plan isn't the best. Small company plans are notorious for their limited options and high costs.

Here's when you should think about leaving your 401(k) plan:
- All your investment options cost 1% or more. The average total expense ratio for stock funds in 401(k) plans has dropped to 0.54%, so if you're paying a lot more than that, it may be time to move on.
- You can't (or don't want to) transfer to your new employer's plan. If the new plan isn't any better, it doesn't accept transfers or just doesn't exist. Many companies don't offer 401(k)s—then a rollover to an IRA could be a reasonable choice as long as you pick a low-cost option.

What a rollover can cost you? Before you pull the trigger on an IRA rollover, you need to understand the other disadvantages, which are numerous.

- No loans. You can't borrow from your IRA for more than 60 days once a year without incurring taxes and penalties. If you can roll your old 401(k) into your new employer's plan, though, you typically can take out loans and pay yourself back.
- No early access. You normally can't tap your IRA before age 59½ without penalty, but money can be taken from 401(k)s penalty-free starting at age 55 if you leave your job.
- Less creditor protection. Your 401(k) has unlimited protection in bankruptcy court and against creditors' claims. Your IRA's bankruptcy exemption tops out at $1,283,025, and protection from creditors' claims varies by state.
- A huge tax trap with company stock. Roll your company stock over into an IRA, and you're giving up a big potential tax break since withdrawals will be taxed as ordinary income. If you instead transfer your company shares to a taxable account when you leave your job, you'll owe income tax on the stocks' original cost, but any subsequent growth can get favorable long-term capital gains treatment. The rest of your 401(k) can be rolled into another employer's 401(k) or to an IRA. Ask your tax pro how to take advantage of this "net unrealized appreciation," or NUA, feature.
- A chance to put off required minimum distributions. IRA money must start coming out of your account after you turn 70½. If you're still working at that age, though, you don't have to begin distributions from your current employer's 401(k) plan until you retire.

If you need help managing your 401(k)/IRA decisions, you might turn to a retirement planner.

Question 57: Do you understand how Required Minimum Distributions (RMD) from your qualified retirement accounts impact your income and taxes, and the penalties for missing a withdrawal?

What the Research Says: If you decide to wait before taking withdrawals from your employer-sponsored retirement plan or traditional IRA, you should understand the required minimum distribution rules imposed by the IRS. These requirements are designed to ensure that you do not defer the taxes indefinitely.

Generally, you must begin taking RMDs by age 72. If you're still employed, you may be able to delay minimum distributions from your current employer's plan until after you retire. But you still must take minimum distributions from other tax-deferred accounts. (Roth IRAs and annuities are an exception.) Your first distribution must be taken no later than April 1 of the year following the year you turn 72. After that first distribution, annual distributions must be taken by December 31 each year. You'll want to think carefully about the timing of your first distribution. What if you do not take the required minimum amount in any given year? Try not to make this mistake, as Uncle Sam does not look favorably on this oversight. Failure to take the required minimum distribution could result in a penalty tax of 50% of the amount that should have been withdrawn. This federal income tax penalty is imposed regardless of the distribution method you choose. The right retirement plan can make sure you stay on top of our RMDs every year and help you manage the tax implications as well.

Taxes in Retirement

Question 58: Do you understand how taxable, tax-deferred, and tax-free wealth buckets work, and your drawdown strategy to maximize after-tax income?

What the Research Says: As you prepare for and enter retirement, you'll want to reduce your taxes to the greatest extent possible. Yes, retirees do in fact pay taxes in retirement. And if you plan right, you can significantly reduce your tax burden in retirement. There are three tax buckets with which you'll strategically place your assets and implement a tax-efficient strategy to withdraw from each of those buckets. A sophisticated tax analysis software and a retirement planner who is tax savvy can help optimize your drawdown strategy.

The **Taxable** bucket generally includes any type of investment for which you receive a 1099 on an annual basis. These funds receive no special tax treatment, and you will typically be taxed on interest and dividends as they are paid, in addition to any gains you make upon the sale of investments in this bucket.

The **Tax-Deferred** bucket includes any retirement accounts to which you have contributed money on a tax-deductible or pre-tax basis, such as most IRAs, 401(k)s, 403(b)s, and others. These accounts typically allow for tax-deferred growth, which means that you are not taxed on income or gains as they occur, but when you eventually take retirement income, the funds you withdraw will be taxed as ordinary income.

Finally, the **Tax-Free** bucket includes accounts to which you contribute after-tax money, such as Roth IRAs, Roth 401(k)s, and others. You do not get any special tax breaks upfront in this bucket, but all contributions and growth can be withdrawn income-tax-free for qualified reasons (which is generally once you are at least 59½ years old and the account has been established for at least 5 years).

Each of these different buckets has its own unique characteristics. Some are more suited for certain needs than others, so it is important to plan accordingly. Most financial professionals would probably agree that the Taxable bucket is the least tax-efficient place to grow a retirement nest egg. Not only do you pay taxes on any interest and dividends each year, but you may also owe capital gains taxes upon selling an investment.

As for the other two buckets, Tax-Deferred and Tax-Free, retirement professionals differ in opinion as to which is better to use. Why? Which bucket to use depends in part upon what will happen in the future. In order to use the different buckets most efficiently, we believe you should not only understand how much you are paying in income taxes while contributing, but also what your income taxes may be in the future when withdrawing from the accounts. Based on the income sources you anticipate being available to you in retirement, you may be able to estimate what your future income taxes will be; however, there is the possibility (and some experts say probability) that income tax rates may increase in the future.

If you were able to predict your future tax bracket, and your income tax rates were going to be lower in retirement than they are now, it may make sense to invest in a tax-deferred account during your higher income-earning years and claim the deduction to reduce your current taxable income. The intent then would be that when you begin taking an income stream from this tax-deferred account in the future/retirement, you would pay a lower rate of income taxes upon withdrawal than you would have owed earlier if you hadn't been able to claim the initial deduction.

However, if you believe that your income will be higher in retirement or that tax rates will increase, it may make sense to invest in a tax-free account during your earning years (and pay taxes on the funds upfront) so that you can withdraw funds in retirement tax-free. Unfortunately, there is no crystal ball available to know what the future will hold. Some investors choose to hedge their bets and invest in both buckets, giving them flexibility and tax diversification in their retirement years. A retirement planner well versed in tax strategy can help you make the best choices for your goals.

Question 59: Do you understand when and how to convert to Roth IRAs and the effect it will have on reducing your taxes?

What the Research Says: A Roth IRA is a special retirement account where you pay taxes on money going into your account and then all future withdrawals are tax-free. Roth IRAs are best when you think your taxes will be higher in retirement than they are right now. They can be especially good for young savers or in years when you don't have much other income.

Converting a portion of a traditional IRA into a Roth IRA is a good idea this year if you have a big tax deduction this year and your marginal tax rate is lower than normal. If you have money in a traditional IRA, any withdrawals are going to be taxable. A useful tax rule-of-thumb is to take withdrawals from these plans at a lower-than-normal tax rate. If you do not need withdrawals to live on, convert it to a Roth IRA (and pay taxes at the low rate) and future earnings are now tax-free.

Roth IRA contributions are made on an after-tax basis. However, keep in mind that your eligibility to contribute to a Roth IRA is based on your income level. The maximum total annual contribution for all your IRAs combined is $6,000 if you're under age 50 and $7,000 if you're age 50 or older. Below you will find a breakdown of the 2023 updates to the Roth IRA contribution income limits:

Deductible IRA Limits and Roth Contribution Eligibility - 2023	DEDUCTIBLE IRA INCOME LIMITS				ROTH IRA INCOME LIMITS	
	If you/spouse ARE covered by an employer retirement plan at any point during the year		If you/spouse are NOT covered by an employer retirement plan at any point during the year		Roth IRA Contribution Eligibility	
Deduction or Contribution	Single	Married filing jointly	Single/married filing jointly (neither spouse covered)	Married filing jointly (one spouse covered)	Single	Married filing jointly
Full	$73,000 or less	$116,000 or less	Any	$218,000 or less	Under 138,000	Under $218,000
Partial deduction (IRA) or contribution (Roth IRA)	More than $73,000 and less than $83,000	More than $116,000 and less than $136,000		More than $218,000 and less than $228,000	138,000	218,000
Non-deductible (IRA) or not eligible (Roth IRA)	Above $83,000	Above $136,000		Above $228,000	153,000	228,000

Tax Filing Status & Modified Adjusted Gross Income Limits

Traditional and Roth IRA limits	Projected 2023	2022
Traditional IRA deduction limits (IRC §§ 219(b)(5) and 219(g)(3)(B))		
IRA maximum deductible amount	$6,500	$6,000
IRA catch-up contribution limit*	1,000	1,000
Modified AGI threshold for determining deductible IRA contributions for active participants in qualified plans		
Married filing jointly or qualifying widow(er)	116,000	109,000
Married filing separately*	0	0
Single or head of household	73,000	68,000
Spouse (but not taxpayer making IRA contribution) is active participant	218,000	204,000
Roth IRA contribution limits (IRC § 408A(c)(3)(B)(ii))		
AGI for determining maximum Roth IRA contribution		
Married filing jointly or qualifying widow(er)	218,000	204,000
Married filing separately*	0	0
Other filing status	138,000	129,000

* Limit is not adjusted for cost-of-living changes.

Question 60: Do you understand how a Health Saving Account (HSA) works and how it acts as a fourth wealth bucket to reduce taxes?

What the Research Says: According to Investopedia, it has become ingrained in us to max out our 401(k) plan or similar workplace-defined contribution plan as the best way to save for retirement.[43] This is certainly good advice. However, in recent years, another retirement savings vehicle (as well as a 4th tax bucket) has come about that might be superior to the 401(k): a health savings account (HSA).

Health savings accounts (HSAs) are tax-advantaged savings accounts designed to help people who have high-deductible health plans (HDHPs) with paying for out-of-pocket medical expenses. While these accounts have been available since 2004, too few eligible Americans are taking advantage of them.

---

[43] Tim Parker, "Maxing Out Your 401(k) and What to Do Next," Investopedia, https://www.investopedia.com/articles/personal-finance/082615/maxing-out-your-401k-profitable-heres-why.asp.

2023 Limits

	2022	2023
HSA Contribution Limits	Self-only: $3,650 Family: $7,300	Self-only: $3,850 Family: $7,750
HDHP (self-only coverage)	Min deductible: $1,400 Max out-of-pocket: $7,050	Min deductible: $1,500 Max out-of-pocket: $7,500
HDHP (family coverage)	Min deductible: $2,800 Max out-of-pocket: $14,100	Min deductible: $3,000 Max out-of-pocket: $15,000
EBHRA Contribution Limits	$1,800	$1,950

According to a July 2015 report from the Employee Benefit Research Institute (EBRI), about 17 million people had HSA-eligible health insurance plans in 2014, but only 13.8 million of that number had opened an HSA. An April 2018 survey of its member insurers by America's Health Insurance Plans (AHIP) reported 21.8 million HSA enrollees in 52 HDHP plans in 2017, up from 20.2 million the previous year. These types of health plans are offered by about 43% of employers right now. EBRI found that virtually no one contributes the maximum, and nearly everyone takes current distributions to pay for medical expenses.

All of this means that consumers who have HSAs—as well as consumers who are eligible for HSAs but haven't opened one—are missing out on an incredible option for funding their later years. It's time to start a new trend. Talk to a retirement planner about how to integrate HSAs into your overall retirement plan and save a lot on taxes.

Key Takeaways:

- The high-deductible health plan you need to qualify for an HSA may be more budget-friendly than it seems because premiums are so low.
- Unlike a Flexible Spending Account, your HSA money is yours forever, and it's portable.
- You can contribute to an HSA until age 65, even when you're not working.
- Invest your HSA money; don't just leave it in a savings account.
- Keep receipts for unreimbursed medical expenses since you got your HSA. You can use them to get tax-free funds from your account.

Question 61: Do you understand what your marginal federal and state income tax rate will be in retirement?

What the Research Says: While you're contributing to your retirement account, you'll want to understand your marginal tax rate. This is the tax rate you pay on each additional dollar of income...the next dollar that you contribute to your retirement account would normally be taxed at the marginal tax rate.

For example, if you are single with a taxable annual income of $50,000, you are in the 25% marginal tax bracket. Using a tax calculator, your effective tax rate would be less than 17% since only the income of $36,900, or $13,100, would be taxed at the 25% rate. The balance would be taxed at 15% or less. However, if you contribute $7,000 to a 401(k) plan pre-tax, all of it would normally be taxed at the 25% rate.

When you take money out of your 401(k) in retirement, some of your income won't be taxed because of standard deductions (in this case $1,550) and exemptions. The first $9,075 of taxable income would be taxed at 10%. The next bucket of income up to $36,900 would be taxed at 15%. Only the income over $36,900 would be taxed at the 25% rate. Unless you have a big pension, your 401(k) contributions will likely be taxed at lower rates. You should also use the lower effective rate when you've estimated how much of your retirement income will go to taxes. It's not necessary to use the higher marginal rate. The outcome might make you believe retirement can never actually happen.

Question 62: Do you understand that the debt held by the United States is expected to break historical records by the 2030s (surpassing 100% of GDP), and that your future tax rates are likely to increase?

What the Research Says: The single biggest threat to your retirement and your security may be taxes. With our national debt at all-time highs of more than $22 trillion dollars, do you believe taxes will be able to stay at all-time lows? Over the last 100 years, the highest tax rate has averaged 61%. Today, our top tax rate is 39.6%, meaning that taxes are discounted by more than 20% relative to the last 100 years. Couple this with the nearly 10,000 baby boomers retiring every day, which is taxing our Social Security system and creating necessary changes by 2034.

The latest projection has the combined Social Security trust funds that pay retirement and disability benefits running out of cash reserves (of $2.8 trillion) by 2034. But that wouldn't leave Social Security bankrupt and unable to pay any benefits. Even if Congress does nothing to shore up the system by 2034, Social Security will be able to pay out 79% of promised benefits until 2090. Would raising taxes be one solution to help fund the Social Security shortfall? Many people believe that taxes absolutely *must* go up. By how much and by when is the question. So, you must ask yourself, "Does it make sense to defer taxes during this super low tax period?" The answer is probably somewhere in the middle, deferring some and paying some in different savings vehicles. A retirement planner can help you determine the right mix of taxable, tax-free, and tax-deferred savings and investment vehicles you're comfortable with, as no one knows for sure where taxes will be when they retire.

Question 63: Do you understand the importance of reviewing your financial strategies in light of the 2017 Tax Cut and Jobs Act (expiring in 2025) to make sure you're using every opportunity to lower your taxes during this limited window?
What the Research Says: The Tax Cuts and Jobs Act of 2017 made several significant changes to the individual income tax, including reforms to itemized deductions and the alternative minimum tax, an expanded standard deduction and child tax credit, and lower marginal tax rates across brackets.

- These changes simplify the individual income tax for millions of households, as 28.5 million filers would be better off taking the newly expanded standard deduction, instead of itemizing various deductions, reducing compliance costs.
- The Internal Revenue Service estimates the average time to complete an individual tax return will decrease by 4–7%. Converting this to dollar terms, we estimate compliance savings could range from $3.1 billion to $5.4 billion.
- Under the new tax law, new limits apply to some itemized deductions, including deductions for state and local taxes paid and mortgage interest, which broadens the tax base and reduces distortions in the tax code.
- The individual income tax changes are scheduled to expire after December 31, 2025.
- It's recommended that you speak to a qualified tax specialist to make sure you are taking proper advantage of these changes.

Insurance

Question 64: Do you understand the benefits of cash value life insurance?
What the Research Says: Like annuities, earnings are not taxed inside a life insurance policy. The earnings are never taxed if the benefit is paid out as a death benefit, and premiums can be withdrawn without income tax consequences during the insured's lifetime. Cash-value life insurance is intended to stay in force throughout life—although policies mature at a particular age (newer policies mature at 120). This contrasts with term insurance that expires after a term of years. Cash value policies typically allow for loans as a way to access cash value if needed. Cash-value life insurance will have higher premiums than term insurance because there is both a death benefit and a cash value that can be accessed during the insured's lifetime.

Question 65: Do you understand the benefits of an Index Universal Life (IUL) policy?

What the Research Says: According to Investopedia, Indexed Universal Life insurance is something of a hybrid vehicle.[44] Like any whole life insurance product, it guarantees a payout upon death. And, like other types of universal life insurance, IUL holds cash value that goes up over time as premiums are paid.

IUL policies give you the flexibility of adjustable life insurance premiums and face value and an opportunity to increase cash value, without the inherent downside risk of investing in the equities market. These policies aren't for everyone, but the combination of flexibility and investment growth may be a good fit for you. Pros of an IUL Policy:

- Low price: The policyholder bears the risk, so the premiums are low.
- Cash value accumulation: Amounts credited to the cash value grow tax deferred. The cash value can pay the insurance premiums, allowing the policyholder to reduce or stop making out-of-pocket premiums payments.
- Flexibility: The policyholder controls the amount risked in indexed accounts vs. a fixed account, and the death benefit amounts can be adjusted as needed. Most IUL policies offer a host of optional riders, from death benefit guarantees to no-lapse guarantees.
- Death benefit: This benefit is permanent, is not subject to income or death taxes and is not required to go through probate.
- Less risky: The policy is not directly invested in the stock market, thus reducing risk.
- Easier distribution: The cash value in IUL policies can be accessed at any time without penalty, regardless of a person's age.
- Unlimited contribution: IUL policies have no limitations on annual contributions.

Cons of an IUL Policy:

- Caps on accumulation percentages: Insurance companies sometimes set a maximum participation rate that is less than 100%.
- Better for larger face amounts: Smaller face values don't offer much advantage over regular universal life policies.
- Based on an equity index: If the index goes down, no interest is credited to the cash value (some policies offer a low guaranteed rate over a longer period). Investment vehicles use market indexes as a benchmark for performance. Their goal is normally to outperform the index. With the IUL, the goal is to profit from upward movements in the index.

---

[44] Kimberly Rotter, "Pros & Cons of Indexed Universal Life Insurance," Investopedia, https://www.investopedia.com/articles/personal-finance/070215/pros-cons-indexed-universal-life-insurance.asp#:~:text=IUL%2C%20also%20known%20as%20equity,time%2C%20as%20premiums%20are%20paid.

The Bottom Line on IULs: While not for everyone, indexed universal life insurance policies are a viable option for people looking for the security of a fixed universal life policy and the interest-earning potential of a variable policy.[45]

Question 66: Do you understand whether you have proper life insurance coverages based on your age?
What the Research Says: A qualified retirement planner can help you determine if you're under-insured, over-insured, or don't need life insurance at all based on your situation. It may seem counterproductive to give up having life insurance after so long, but the truth may be that you no longer need it. If you have no income to replace, very little debt, a self-sufficient family, and no pricey concerns around settling your estate, there's a good chance that you can say goodbye to that policy. As far as estate planning goes, you could well need a different type of policy or major changes to your current one anyway.

Question 67: Do you understand that disability and liability insurances are important to consider for covering your risks in these areas?
What the Research Says: While considering your life insurance needs as you approach and enter retirement, it's important to consider your needs for disability and liability insurance. While most people see the obvious benefits of life insurance or health insurance, disability insurance is often overlooked. But it's just as important a part of your financial plan as other types of insurance. Disability insurance ensures that you have income coming in even if you're sick or injured to protect all your financial plans. The short answer to the question "Do you need disability insurance?" is yes.

If you work, have people relying on your income, and aren't financially able to go years, or even just months, without a paycheck, you should consider disability insurance.
Why do you need it? Because most people are unprotected and at risk of not being able to pay bills or support their families.
Consider the following:

- Over 25% of American workers experience a long-term disability longer than three months at some point in their careers.
- 69% of workers have no long-term disability insurance coverage.
- 62% of all US bankruptcies and more than 50% of all mortgage foreclosures stem from an illness or injury-related medical issues.

---

[45] Stephanie Powers, "Indexed Universal Life (IUL) Insurance," Investopedia, https://www.investopedia.com/articles/insurance/09/indexed-universal-life-insurance.asp.

You may think that disability insurance is just for accidents and that you're not at risk if you don't work a dangerous job. However, 90% of long-term disabilities result from illness rather than accident, meaning they can affect you no matter what you do for work. Even white-collar professions like doctors and lawyers need disability insurance. In fact, because of the expensive educational investments in these fields, they benefit even more from disability coverage.

If you don't have disability insurance, you risk not being able to cover everyday expenses, pay regular bills, or keep up with your larger financial plan. Disability insurance protects your most valuable asset—your ability to earn an income—and it should be considered a part of every financial safety net.[46]

Healthcare in Retirement

Question 68: Do you understand how Medicare works?
What the Research Says: The Medicare maze is quite complicated and will require some outside advice (unless of course, you have a burning desire to learn all about Medicare). Medicare is the national health insurance program to which all Social Security recipients who are either over 65 years of age or permanently disabled are eligible. In addition, individuals receiving railroad retirement benefits and individuals suffering from the end-stage renal disease are eligible to receive Medicare benefits.

Medicare is *not* a welfare program and should not be confused with Medicaid. The income and assets of a Medicare beneficiary are *not* a consideration in determining eligibility or benefits payment. Medicare is a national program and procedures should *not* vary significantly from state to state. Coverage under Medicare is like that provided by private insurance companies—it pays a portion of the cost of medical care. Often, deductibles and coinsurance (partial payment of initial and subsequent costs) are required of the beneficiary. Medicare has two substantive coverage components, Part A and Part B. Part A covers inpatient hospital care, hospice care, inpatient care in a skilled nursing facility, and home health care services. Part B covers medical care and services provided by doctors and other medical practitioners, home health care, durable medical equipment, and some outpatient care and home health services.[47]

Question 69: Do you understand what your Medicare choices are?
What the Research Says: When you first enroll in Medicare and during certain times of the year, you can choose how you get your Medicare coverage. There are two main ways to get your Medicare coverage: Original Medicare (Part A and Part B) or a Medicare Advantage Plan

---

[46] Colin Lalley, "Do I Need Disability Insurance?" *Policygenius*, March 29, 2018, https://www.policygenius.com/disability-insurance/learn/do-i-need-disability-insurance/.
[47] *Medicare Hospice Benefits*, https://www.medicare.gov/Pubs/pdf/02154-medicare-hospice-benefits.pdf.

(Part C). Some people need to get additional coverage, like Medicare prescription drug coverage or Medicare Supplement Insurance (Medigap).

Here are the steps/decisions you'll need to make:
> Step 1: Decide whether you want Original Medicare or a Medicare Advantage Plan (like an HMO/PPO).
> Step 2: Decide whether you want prescription drug coverage (Part D).
> Step 3: Decide whether you want supplemental coverage.

Other options:
- In addition to Original Medicare or a Medicare Advantage Plan, you may be able to join other types of Medicare health plans.
- You may be able to save money or have other choices if you have limited income and resources.
- You may also have other coverage, like employer or union, military, or veterans' benefits.

Question 70: Do you understand the estimated total amount of out-of-pocket costs for health care in retirement?

What the Research Says: If you are like most Americans, health care is expected to be one of your largest expenses in retirement, after housing and transportation costs. But unlike your parents' generation, you won't likely have access to employer- or union-sponsored retiree health benefits. So, health care costs will likely consume a larger portion of your retirement budget—and you need to plan for that. Health care is creating a "retirement cost gap" for many pre-retirees.

How much should you plan to pay in health care costs after you retire? According to the Fidelity Retiree Health Care Cost Estimate, an average retired couple age 65 in 2022 may need approximately $315,000 saved (after tax) to cover health care expenses in retirement.[48] Of course, the amount you'll need will depend on when and where you retire, how healthy you are, and how long you live. The amount you need will also depend on which accounts you use to pay for health care, e.g., 401(k), HSA, IRA, or taxable accounts; your tax rates in retirement; and potentially even your gross income.

Tip: If you're still working and your employer offers an HSA-eligible health plan, consider enrolling and contributing to a health savings account (HSA). An HSA can help you save tax-efficiently for health care costs in retirement. You can save pre-tax dollars (and possibly collect employer contributions), which have the potential to grow and be withdrawn tax-free for federal and state tax purposes if used for qualified medical expenses.

---

[48] *2022 Retiree Health Care Cost Estimate*, Fidelity Investments, https://s2.q4cdn.com/997146844/files/doc_news/archive/b6f07a26-3aa9-4a98-af00-b1b783cfd552.pdf.

Question 71: Do you understand the cost of prescription drugs in retirement and their impact on my finances?
What the Research Says: Since its inception in 2006, the Medicare Part D prescription drug benefit has helped improve the affordability of medications for millions of people with Medicare. Yet many beneficiaries continue to face high out-of-pocket costs for their medications. Prescription drugs accounted for $1 in every $5 that Medicare beneficiaries spent out-of-pocket on healthcare services in 2016, not including premiums, according to a new report by the Kaiser Family Foundation.[49]

One of the most valuable things you can do is check the Medicare health and drug plan choices every year and switch plans when it makes sense to do so. During Medicare Open Enrollment, which runs from October 15 to December 7 every year, Medicare beneficiaries can switch prescription drug plans and enroll in or switch Medicare Advantage plans.

Question 72: Do you understand what your monthly premiums for Medicare Part B will be and when they will be deducted?
What the Research Says: Using Medicare benefit guidance/consultants you'll be able to get an accurate estimate of your Medicare Part B premiums and calculate these costs into your retirement income/expense summary.

Question 73: Do you understand the importance of including health care expenses in your retirement income projection?
What the Research Says: It's important to consider your health care costs in your retirement income projection since the average projected out-of-pocket costs exceed $280,000 per couple. This is not a retirement expense you can afford to overlook.

Long-Term Care

Question 74: Do you understand the risk of long-term care (LTC) incidents?
What the Research Says: According to the National Clearinghouse for Long Term Care Information, a person's lifetime risk of needing long-term care services in their lifetime is 1 out of 2; that's a 50% risk. As age increases, so does the likelihood of needing long-term care. 70% of people over the age of 65 will require some type of long-term care service during their lifetime. Remember that long-term care is something you may need before 65 years of age; about 50% of people who currently need long-term care services are under the age of 65.

---

[49] "10 Essential Facts About Medicare and Prescription Drug Spending," KFF.org, Kaiser Family Foundation, January 29, 2019, https://www.kff.org/infographic/10-essential-facts-about-medicare-and-prescription-drug-spending/.

Let's compare the risk:

- Automobile accident is 1 out of 240 (0.4%)
- Fire damaging your home is 1 out of 1,200 (0.08%)
- Missing 90 days of work due to a disability is just under 1 in 3 (33%)
- Needing long-term care assistance in your lifetime is 1 out of 2 (50%)

A long-term care policy can help you:

- Maintain your financial independence
- Preserve the wealth you've worked so hard for over your lifetime
- Avoid burdening family and friends with your care
- Protect your ability to remain independent
- Have access to quality care.

Question 75: Do you understand the average annual cost of long-term care in a nursing home?
What the Research Says: Genworth's Cost of Care survey in 2021 reveals that in the United States, a private room in a nursing home costs an average of $108,405/year. In Massachusetts, the cost is over $167,000. In Connecticut, it's over $182,000/year for 2022.[50]

Wondering who pays for the majority of long-term care expenses provided in nursing homes? Many do not realize that most institutional care is paid for by Medicaid. Medicaid only pays for care once an individual has essentially run out of assets, and care is limited to those institutions that take Medicaid and have beds available. This is a public policy concern as well, as the Medicaid system is really taxed by these costs, which are likely to continue to grow as baby boomers age.

Question 76: Do you understand long-term care policy costs?
What the Research Says: The cost of long-term care insurance will depend on the coverage you choose. Your premium is based in part on your age, the length of time you want to be covered for care, your health, the elimination period, and the maximum dollar amount you will be reimbursed for care.

In 2022, you can expect to pay anywhere from $79 to $533 per month for a long-term care insurance policy. These premiums, however, vary greatly based on age, gender, health, and the coverage amount of the policy.[51] That puts the coverage out of reach for many Americans. One

---

[50] "Cost of Care Survey," Genworth, https://www.genworth.com/aging-and-you/finances/cost-of-care.html.
[51] Ellen Stark, "5 Things You Should Know about Long-Term Care Insurance," *AARP Bulletin*, March 1, 2018, https://www.aarp.org/caregiving/financial-legal/info-2018/long-term-care-insurance-fd.html.

bright spot for spouses: discounts for couples are common, typically 30% off the price of policies bought separately.

Question 77: Do you understand the tax advantages of buying long-term care insurance?
What the Research Says: When purchasing a long-term care insurance policy, you'll have access to some tax advantages if you itemize deductions, especially as you get older. Some state and federal tax codes let you count part or all long-term care insurance premiums as medical expenses, which are tax-deductible if they meet a certain threshold. The limits for the number of premiums you can deduct increase with your age.[52]

2021 Long-Term Care Deductible Limits per Individual

Attained age before end of taxable year	2021 limit (and limit in 2020)
40 or younger	$450 ($430)
Ages 41 to 50	$850 ($810)
Ages 51 to 60	$1,690 ($1,630)
Ages 61 to 70	$4,520 ($4,350)
Age 71 and older	$5,640 ($5,430)

Source: IRS

Only premiums for tax-qualified long-term care insurance policies count as medical expenses. Such policies must meet certain federal standards and be labeled as tax qualified. Ask your retirement planner whether a policy is tax-qualified if you're not sure.

Question 78: Do you understand what long-term care insurance is intended to cover?
What the Research Says: Long-term care insurance is intended to provide a funding vehicle for custodial and semi-skilled nursing care, which is generally not covered by Medicare and other health insurance. Custodial care for someone with Alzheimer's is one common example of when benefits would be paid out. Long-term care insurance reduces the burden on family members and helps make sure that the retiree is less likely to end up spending down all their resources at the end of their life. It also, in most cases, gives the family more options for where and how care is provided.

---

[52] "Long Term Care Insurance Tax-Deductibility Rues – TTC Tax Rules," *Consumer's Information Center*, American Association for Long-Term Care Insurance, https://www.aaltci.org/long-term-care-insurance/learning-center/tax-for-business.php.

Question 79: Do you understand the importance of calculating long-term care expenses in your retirement income projection?
What the Research Says: Like health care expenses, you'll want to make sure that you have accounted for long-term care expenses or insurance in your income projection.

Question 80: Do you understand the options to fund a long-term care policy?
What the Research Says: If your assets are few, you may eventually be able to cover LTC costs via Medicaid, available only if you're impoverished; if you have lots of money saved, you likely can pay for future care out of pocket. But weigh factors other than cash: Do you have home equity you could tap into? Do you have children who can be counted on to pitch in? Do you have a family history of dementia that puts you at higher risk of needing care?

Some people tap into the benefits of a Home Equity Conversion Loan (HECM), or reverse mortgage, as a buffer against a long-term care incident. If you're pulling less than 4% out of your savings each year for living expenses, you may be comfortable going without insurance altogether. In this case, though, you'll need to plan for a possible LTC expense.

College Funding

Question 81: Do you understand how you'll fund your child's college education?
What the Research Says: There are a number of ways to fund your child's college education. If you start early, know your investment vehicle alternatives, develop a plan, and invest wisely and regularly, it is possible to pay for some or all of your child's college education. When trying to come up with the money for your child's college education, a combination of investment vehicles and financing methods will probably work best. Be sure to take advantage of any tax-deductible or tax-deferred methods that you're eligible for.

Some of the best investment options for college savings include:

- Roth IRA: If you'll be 59½ when your child is in college, a Roth IRA may be an attractive investment vehicle, because the investments will grow tax-free, and withdrawals will also be tax-free (assuming you've had the account for at least five years). You can withdraw up to $10,000 tax and penalty-free before age 59½, as long as the money is used for qualified education expenses.
- Coverdell Education Savings Account (formerly known as an Education IRA): While contributions to a Coverdell ESA are not tax-deductible (meaning you must pay taxes on the money now), the account's value will grow tax-free and distributions from the account are tax-free when used for qualified education expenses for the designated beneficiary. The primary downside to Coverdell ESAs is that there is a low limit of $2,000 on annual contributions, and families with an adjusted gross income (AGI) above the limit cannot participate. Once your child turns 18, you can't make any new contributions

to the plan. All Coverdell ESA savings must be used before your child turns 30; otherwise, you'll pay a stiff tax penalty on any remaining balance.[53]

Question 82: Do you understand how a 529 plan works for college savings?
What the Research Says: State College Savings Plans (529 plans) give you the opportunity to earn stock-market returns on college savings that you don't need for several years. Contributions grow tax-deferred until the money is used to pay for college, then earnings are taxed at the student's tax rate, another attractive benefit as the student's tax rate is generally lower than their parents'. If the money isn't used for qualified education expenses, however, there can be a penalty of 10% to 15% of your accumulated earnings or 1% of the account balance. So, you want to be sure not to over-save into a 529 Plan. For most states' 529 plans, there is essentially no annual contribution limit, but these plans do have a lifetime contribution limit. The limit varies by plan.

Prepaid Tuition Plans: These plans are essentially another type of 529 plan, but unlike 529 plans, the state takes on much of the risk in the prepaid plan. These state-run plans are particularly attractive as college tuition rates are rising around 10% a year. But they come with some major limitations. First, the invested funds can be used only for tuition and fees (not room and board or other expenses) at in-state public universities. Using the money for any other purpose or college will result in paying penalties. Second, prepaid tuition plans limit your growth to the rate of public college tuition increases in your state. So, when tuition increases level off at 4–5%, these plans are no longer very attractive vehicles for financing a college education.[54]

Question 83: Do you understand the trade-offs between funding college education vs. saving for retirement?
What the Research Says: For parents, who haven't set aside enough money to cover their kid's college bills, and there are many, there's a temptation to forego saving for your own retirement and instead send money to a big-name college.

Many parents stretch themselves thin paying for their children's college education and even forgoing saving for retirement altogether. This is a slippery slope. Some justify this choice by telling themselves it's a temporary break from saving for their own future. The fact of the matter is that this choice could have a permanent negative effect on your future. Consider your choices carefully and understand the trade-offs.

---

[53] Ken Clark, "A Beginner's Guide to the Coverdell ESA," The Balance, March 27, 2020, https://www.thebalance.com/beginners-guide-to-coverdell-esas-4060459.
[54] "Cutting College Costs," *The SmartStudent™ Guide to Financial Aid*, https://www.finaid.org/questions/cuttingcollegecosts.phtml.

Parents Plan to Raid Retirement to Pay for College
According to college education lender Sallie Mae, parents of college students pay 28% of their children's college expenses from their own income and savings. This means that parents' savings, including their retirement savings plans, are more than likely being used to fund their kid's college degrees.

In addition, the study found that less than half of parents with kids younger than 6-years old would consider using their retirement for college, while 74% of families with teens would pay for college with retirement funds! As kids approach college age, parents become even more open to the idea of using their nest eggs to pay for college![55] So, what's the issue? Taking your retirement funds may cover the cost of education, but at what cost to you?

Consider these top issues:
- You'll significantly reduce your retirement savings and miss out on the growth of that fund. The average cost of tuition and fees to attend a ranked public college in state is about 74% less than the average sticker price at a private college, at $10,423 for the 2022-2023 year compared with $39,723, respectively, U.S. News data shows.[56]
- Withdrawals from defined-contribution plans (such as 401(k)s) count as taxable income, which can raise your taxes and reduce your child's eligibility for financial aid next year. There are also withdrawal penalties, depending on your plan, to consider.
- If you are younger than 59½ and have the ability to borrow the funds from your 401(k), you'll have to pay back the loan with interest within five years—or immediately if you change employers or lose your job.

Reducing Your Retirement Savings Can Come Back to Bite the Kids
If you empty out your retirement savings for Johnny's college bill or you choose not to save the recommended 15%/month in your 401(k), you could end-up being reliant on him in retirement! There are other, smarter options You and your student (and hopefully you make your student do most of the work) should think about. Please consider them. There are scholarships, grants, part-time jobs, work-study, and going to a less-expensive school or doing two years at a community college and then transferring to a more expensive college for the second two years. Most experts agree that choosing your retirement plan over your kids' college tuition doesn't make you a bad parent; it makes you a responsible parent.

---

[55] "How America Saves for College 2013: A National Study by Sallie Mae and Ipsos," Sallie Mae, https://news.salliemae.com/research-tools/america-saves-2013#:~:text=How%20America%20Saves%20for%20College%202013%3A%20A%20national%20study%20by,two%20years%20ago%20(60%25).
[56] See the Average College Tuition in 2021-2022 (usnews.com)

Cover Your Monthly Contributions and Then Help Them Out

Assuming you're not behind on retirement savings and you're investing 15% of your income for retirement, feel free to start saving for your kids' college. But make sure to take advantage of retirement savings catch-up provisions first if you're behind and over 50 years old.

Consider picking up a copy of the book, *Debt-Free Degree*.[57] You and your student should read it and consider the options that don't mean giving up your retirement savings.

Estate Planning

Question 84: Do you understand, given your financial and family situation, how a will and trust could protect you and your estate?

What the Research Says: Your estate comprises all the assets you own. This includes bank accounts, investments such as stocks and bonds, real estate, business interests, life insurance policies, and other personal property and valuables, such as automobiles, jewelry, and artwork. You don't have to own a mansion on the hill to have an estate, and you don't need to be wealthy to have a need for estate planning.

The three goals of estate planning include:

1. Managing wealth during your lifetime,
2. Distributing assets upon your death, and
3. Maintaining control of your assets.

By taking the necessary steps to conserve your estate, you and your family will:

- Avoid conflicts among your family members. If all your assets are accounted for and your wishes are spelled out in detail, the chance that anyone will contest your estate plans will be reduced.
- Avoid the delays of probate and other proceedings by addressing these issues while you're alive, rather than forcing your heirs to endure some drawn-out procedures after you're gone.
- Avoid some legal and court expenses by having a well-organized estate with properly drafted legal documents.

A will provides instructions detailing how you want your estate to be distributed. A trust allows you to hold assets for the benefit of another; they can help preserve and distribute your estate.

---

[57] Anthony ONeal, *Debt-Free Degree: The Step-by-Step Guide to Getting Your Kid Through College Without Student Loans*, (Ramsey Press, 2019).

A trust is a legal way to set aside assets for a specific purpose. A living trust is created while you are still alive, offering flexibility and control over your estate in the event of incapacitation or death. Here are six benefits of creating a living trust:

1. Avoid Probate
2. Protect privacy
3. Protect from court challenges due to incapacitation
4. Increase flexibility
5. Save money and protect property
6. Allow greater control of assets

There are two important types of trusts: revocable and irrevocable. The former is a trust in which the grantor retains the rights to manage the assets and thus can remove assets from the trust. The latter trust is one in which the grantor relinquishes all rights to the asset. One of the benefits of this is the avoidance of certain taxes at death or removing assets that may otherwise have been used for Medicare proceedings.

Trusts can also be set up to pass funds to charities over time which also carries tax benefits. Other documents that typically make up an estate plan include a power of attorney and a living will. A power of attorney gives a trusted individual the power and authority to act on your behalf in legal and financial matters.

A durable power of attorney enables you to name a trusted individual to act on your behalf even if you become disabled or incapacitated. This person would make investments and other financial decisions that would affect your overall estate until you recover.

A living will, which is different from a standard will, outlines which medical procedures you will allow in the event of a debilitating or chronic illness. Living wills are most often used to authorize termination of artificial life support in the event of a terminal illness.
Note: Laws governing each of these documents can vary significantly from state to state, so it would be wise to become familiar with the laws of your state.[58]

Question 85: Do you understand the importance of having a medical power of attorney in place for yourself, your spouse, and your single children over 18?
What the Research Says: A medical durable power of attorney is another important component of your estate plan that outlines your preferences for forms of medical treatment and gives an individual the authority to make medical decisions for you if you are unable to make them yourself.

---

[58] "Estate Conservation: Preserving Wealth for Your Heirs," Broadridge Investor Communication Solutions, https://www.broadridgeadvisor.com/docs/seminar/estate-conservation-presentationsample.pdf.

Question 86: Do you understand the legal instrument that you could use to limit your long-term care expenses to a max of 60 months?

What the Research Says: By creating a Medicaid Trust. A Medicaid Trust, sometimes erroneously called a Medicare Trust, is an irrevocable trust. It holds the assets of the future nursing home patient. It must be properly worded and have a trustee, which can be your children, another relative, or an independent third party. The Administration on Aging, a division of the US Department of Health and Human Services says, "This is the only kind of trust that is exempt from rules regarding trusts and Medicaid eligibility."[59] To make sure Medicaid will not disallow any assets you include in the trust, you must set it up and transfer assets into it at least five years prior to entering a nursing home or applying for long-term care. This is called a five-year look-back period.

Some people make the big mistake of leaving all assets to family members in a will instead of creating a trust. One big problem with this scenario is that it can create a tremendous gift tax bill. If the same family member received the assets after the parent or grandparent died, there would likely be no tax bill. That is unless the assets were in the multi-millions. Other, perhaps larger, problems arise when the child or grandchild has received the house, the car, and the bank account. Say they are sued. Perhaps they run into a tax problem, die, get divorced, or incur a huge hospital bill. Grandma's home, automobile, and accounts could be confiscated. Those are some additional reasons why a much better option is the Medicaid trust. Moreover, this type of trust is a valuable part of estate planning. It can help you avoid the expensive and time-consuming probate process.[60]

Getting Help

Question 87: Do you understand the different types of "advisors" you may encounter when looking for financial advice?

What the Research Says: There are more than 300,000 "financial advisors and planners" in the United States. 80% of them are men and their average age is 60. The title financial planner or financial advisor is used to describe anyone from an insurance agent to a stockbroker to an investment advisor to a Certified Financial Planner (CFP). And there's no shortage of certifications and acronyms on advisors' business cards. No wonder people are confused when trying to decipher from whom they should get financial or retirement advice from.

---

[59] "Financial Requirements – Assets," https://longtermcare.acl.gov/medicare-medicaid-more/medicaid/medicaid-eligibility/financial-requirements-assets.html.
[60] "Medicaid Trust: Qualify for Government Aid for Nursing Home Cost," Asset Protection Planners, https://www.assetprotectionplanners.com/planning/estate-planning/medicaid-trust/.

Many investors assume that any professionals who refer to themselves as "financial planners" have received certification. Unfortunately, there's no rule governing who can go by the title of financial planner; anyone can set up shop using that title, whether they know anything about finance or have any experience. You're better off sticking with financial planners who have certification by a governing agency, be it state or federal.

Here's a quick overview of the types of advisors and planners who have certifications:

Registered Investment Advisor (RIA): A person or firm who advises individuals on investments and manages their portfolios. RIAs have a fiduciary duty to their clients, which means they have a fundamental obligation to provide investment advice that always acts in their clients' best interests. As the first word of their title indicates, RIAs are required to register either with the Securities and Exchange Commission (SEC) or state securities administrators.
Registered investment advisors seek to offer more holistic financial plans and investing services. They offer very different fee schedules and are typically fee-based by assets under management.

Registered Representatives: Someone who works for a brokerage company and is well versed in investment products including stocks, bonds, and mutual funds. Registered representatives are required to have passed their Series 6 and/or Series 7 exams. They must register with the Financial Industry Regulatory Authority (FINRA) and are governed by suitability standards (which means they ensure an investment is suitable given an investor's investment profile). Registered representatives, also known as stockbrokers, work on commission. Since reps are regulated by FINRA, you can check an advisor's background on FINRA's Central Registration Depository at www.finra.org.

Many financial advisors or planners attain other certifications (some of which are listed below). So, for example, you may meet with someone who is both an RIA and a CFP or an RIA and an insurance agent.

Certified financial planner (CFP): The CFP certification is offered by the CFP Board and is generally considered the gold-standard certification for financial planners. CFPs are always fiduciaries, meaning they are legally required to put their clients' interests ahead of their own at all times.

Chartered financial analyst (CFA): The CFA designation is granted only by the CFA Institute. To gain this certification, advisors must meet significant education and work experience requirements and pass a series of three exams. CFAs have expertise in investment analysis and portfolio management.

Retirement Income Certifications: There are three major retirement income planning certifications that many financial advisors choose to attain. These include Retirement Income

Certified Professional (RICP), Retirement Management Analyst (RMA), and Certified Retirement Counselor (CRC).

Other "advisors" you may have on your team:

Insurance agents: Insurance agents are licensed to sell life insurance and annuity products, within their state. They are typically paid by commission based on the products they sell. Insurance agents are monitored by state insurance commissioners and, in comparison to investment advisors, the standards are significantly lower. There are consumer protection standards in place that protect you from deceptive practices and misrepresentation of products. However, there is no requirement for agents to act in their client's best interests. And remember, that some insurance agents call themselves financial planners leading some consumers to be misled about the full capabilities of the agents. Some financial advisors/planners are also insurance licensed, which we feel is a benefit to you when working with someone on your retirement plan since he or she will be able to offer a potentially balanced view between the two.

Certified public accountant (CPA): While certified public accountants (CPAs) are most often associated with taxes, they can also act as trusted financial advisors.

Personal financial specialist (PFS): Offered by the American Institute of Certified Public Accountants (AICPA), the PFS designation is an "add-on" certification for CPAs. It is intended for CPAs who want to branch out into financial planning and requires that the CPA in question have at least two years of personal financial planning experience, either in business or teaching.

Estate Planning Attorney: There is more to estate planning advice than the preparation of a last will and testament. Attorneys help you prepare for the possibility of mental or physical incapacitation and the need for long-term care. They can also advise clients on ways to ensure that their life's savings and assets are safe from beneficiaries' creditors after your death.

Question 88: Do you understand the criticality of working with an advisor who has either experience or certifications in retirement planning or retirement income planning?
What the Research Says: In addition to the certifications listed above you should discover the advisor's knowledge and expertise in the myriad of retirement topics that are relevant to you. He or she should understand "retirement optimized" strategies that are required in the distribution phase of life (vs. the accumulation phase). This is a special area of focus that requires continuing education and in-depth training. Many traditional financial advisors have not made the commitment to understanding the nuances of retirement.

Question 89: Do you understand the value a "hybrid retirement planner" can offer over a "traditional investment advisor"?

What the Research Says: Historically, the financial services industry has been very siloed and as a result, depending on which type of advisor you meet with, you may get biased information.

- CPAs Prepare Taxes: Typically focused on tax returns, *not* on tax proactive planning
- Insurance Agents: Typically focused on annuities & life insurance
- Investment Advisors: Typically focused on traditional investments

The biases and extremism prevalent in the different silos can harm your retirement. The insurance industry zealots warn people that "you could lose all your money in the market overnight."[61] The investment industry zealots warn people that "insurance and annuities are overpriced and sold by commissioned salespeople who are out to rob you."[62] Meanwhile, most CPAs provide insight into what happened in the past (i.e. last year's tax return) vs. proactive tax planning and retirement tax planning.

To combat this, a new type of advisor has emerged. The Hybrid Retirement Planner offers balanced viewpoints because he or she is registered as both an RIA and a broker and is also licensed to sell insurance products. Good "retirement educated" hybrid planners don't operate in biased extremes. Given proper retirement planning training, they can provide sound guidance on all aspects of a client's financial position, including wealth management and inter-generational transfer. In other words, a hybrid planner is in a position to offer balanced advice that tends to fall in the middle between the extremes of investment advisors who focus on traditional investment strategies and insurance representatives expounding the virtues of guaranteed insurance strategies.

As with all professions, there are many qualified hybrid "retirement planners" who know what they're doing, but there are perhaps even more who call themselves retirement specialists but who don't truly understand the intricacies of retirement planning. Many are still focused on selling products for a commission versus using a research-based investment management process. It takes time to understand and assimilate the vast body of information and research coming out every day that can potentially give a pre-retiree or retiree the best possible retirement outcomes.

Hybrid planners can also offer certain products such as specific types of annuities and long-term care insurance that can only be used for clients via a broker-based program. As well, there are

---

[61] "Wealth Beyond Wall Street: Retirement Planning Solution or Scam," Bank On Yourself, https://www.bankonyourself.com/wealth-beyond-wall-street-radio-ads-facts-myths.html.
[62] Jane Wollman Rusoff, "Why Ken Fisher Hates Annuities," ThinkAdvisor, October 26, 2015, https://www.thinkadvisor.com/2015/10/26/why-ken-fisher-hates-annuities/.

much more robust product offerings through the broker channel versus the advisor channel. This affords the hybrid planner the ability to truly act in the client's best interests and use the proper products, based on research, analysis, and the individualized need of each client. In addition, independent hybrid planners can access many different products and can offer a highly efficient combination of quality and low fees.

Pre-retirees' needs are different than at any other age and are becoming increasingly complex. A hybrid planner with proper retirement planning education and knowledge is better suited to offer a broad range of research-backed advice-driven strategies and solutions to pre-retirees. Hybrid retirement planners are also committed to retirement based on research vs. gut feel or best guesses. When you meet with a retirement planner make sure you ask what academic research he or she uses to base his or her recommendations on, as well as the leading researchers he or she relies on for data, information, and recommended strategies. If the hybrid retirement planner is a true believer in research, he or she will be able to name the top academics who are making significant impacts in the retirement industry.

A note about the difference between an Investment Advisor Representative (IAR) and a stockbroker: For most of the general public, the term fiduciary is misunderstood, with its exact implications on the consumer fuzzy at best. Essentially, a fiduciary is someone whose duties are both ethical and legal. They are bound ethically to act in another person's best interests. IARs (as required by the SEC) have a fiduciary duty to always act in the best interests of their clients.

Professional fiduciaries are heavily regulated by the Securities & Exchange (SEC) and held to certain fiduciary standards to ensure that a client's finances are as secure and protected as possible. A professional fiduciary is required to adhere to policies designed to prevent a client's funds from being misappropriated or poorly managed. Fiduciaries or IARs typically charge a fee to clients for their services and these fees are often based on a percentage of assets under management. IARs (as required by the SEC) have a fiduciary duty to always act in the best interests of their clients.

"So, do financial advisers add value? The research strongly supports that they do, both in terms of improving means and quality of life. But they only add value when we know what to look for when selecting the appropriate partner. Our natural tendencies will be toward excess complexity and flashy marketing, seeking out those who lead with bold claims of esoteric knowledge. What will add much greater richness is a partner who balances deep knowledge with deep rapport. Someone we will listen to when we are scared and who will save us from ourselves; a simple solution to a complex problem."[63] –*Behavioral Alpha: The True Power of Financial Advice,* Daniel Crosby, Ph.D., Nocturne Capital, October 2016

---

[63] Daniel Crosby, "Behavioral Alpha: The True Power of Financial Advice," Barron's, October 17, 2016, https://www.barrons.com/articles/behavioral-alpha-the-true-power-of-financial-advice-1476396872.

Advisor Suitability Test

We suggest you take a quick Advisor suitability self-test to help you determine in which areas you may need outside help. The test will ask about your confidence to manage your financial decisions for retirement in a number of different areas.

1) How confident are you in your current financial plan?
    1-Confident   2-Somewhat Confident   3-Not Confident
2) How confident are you in your retirement plan (savings & investments, taxes, insurance, home equity, healthcare, estate planning)?
    1-Confident   2-Somewhat Confident   3-Not Confident
3) How confident are you in the amount of savings and investments you have for retirement?
    1-Confident   2-Somewhat Confident   3-Not Confident
4) How confident are you in determining your retirement income distribution strategy (while minimizing taxes)?
    1-Confident   2-Somewhat Confident   3-Not Confident
5) How confident are you in making your own short-term and long-term investment decisions (and not making knee-jerk reactions) in market downturns?
    1-Confident   2-Somewhat Confident   3-Not Confident
6) How confident are you in your portfolio allocations to balance growth and protection (right ratio to protect against short term and long-term volatility)?
    1-Confident   2-Somewhat Confident   3-Not Confident
7) How confident are you in determining the right Social Security claiming strategy to maximize your benefit in light of all your other income sources?
    1-Confident   2-Somewhat Confident   3-Not Confident
8) How confident are you in understanding how your home equity can be used in retirement?
    1-Confident   2-Somewhat Confident   3-Not Confident

Total Score_____. If you score anywhere from 16-24, it's likely that a financial/retirement advisor will be able to improve your retirement outcome.

Studies show that working with an advisor is proven to boost confidence, reduce stress and improve overall financial outcomes. A qualified retirement advisor can help you determine an efficient and sustainable income distribution strategy when in retirement. The right advisor can also incorporate tax planning into your overall strategy. Advisors can help you determine the right strategies for saving and investing for retirement, and proper growth/protection as you approach retirement. A retirement advisor can address all of your financial and lifestyle concerns as you prepare for the transition and live in retirement.

_____

Question 90: Do you understand the importance of taking a retirement inventory, determining your retirement readiness, and then finding out how to make your retirement income as efficient and sustainable as possible?

What the Research Says: In an effort to make sure you continue with your retirement education and planning; we suggest you check out the Her Retirement Personalized Readiness Platform. This powerful software gives you an all-in-one retirement planning system designed to assess and fill your gaps in knowledge, preparedness, and guidance. You can learn more at: www.HerRetirement.com/platform

We truly hope that this Her Retirement book has given you some valuable, actionable information about your finances and retirement. It's a lot to unpack, digest, and take action on, but that's the key to everything in life. It's great to get financially literate, but the goal is financial wellness…now and in retirement. Let us know how we can help you do both.

www.HerRetirement.com

ADDENDUM

One to Five Year Countdown to Retirement Checklist

Important dates

- ☐ Confirm your retirement date: _____
- ☐ Date to start taking your retirement income: _____
- ☐ Apply for Social Security benefits online at ssa.gov or by phone at 1-800-772-1213 (allow three months prior to income need)
- ☐ Apply for Medicare either online at ssa.gov or by phone at 1-800-772-1213 (complete three months prior to 65th birthday)

Retirement expectations

- ☐ Consult with your employer regarding retirement date
- ☐ Determine whether you need or want to work in retirement
- ☐ Talk with your employer about remaining on the job in a part-time or consulting position, if desired

Retirement expenses and assets

- ☐ Review your financial inventory
  - Expenses (housing, clothing, food, transportation, taxes, insurance, healthcare) and
  - Estimate healthcare and prescription drug expenses and determine what coverage
  - options are available through your employer or on an individual basis
  - Consider long-term care insurance
- ☐ Re-verify all income sources in retirement (e.g., retirement plan, pension, Social Security, individual retirement account [IRA], income annuity, trust, etc.)
- ☐ Review the investment allocation for retirement funds, including current and former employer-sponsored retirement plans, IRAs and annuities
- ☐ Make an election for any company-provided pension benefits and determine the appropriate retirement plan distribution options
- ☐ Consult with your financial professional or employer's plan administrator if you have retirement savings invested in employer stock to help determine if you are eligible for special tax treatment

Retirement planning

- ☐ Evaluate retirement funds and expenses to create monthly budget
- ☐ Set aside money for short-term living expenses and travel
- ☐ Ensure your retirement income sources and savings will allow you to retire on your target retirement date
- ☐ Consult with your financial professional to create a plan to convert your retirement savings into a sufficient stream of income (your "retirement paycheck") — consider planning for 30 years of retirement income
- ☐ Consider income management vehicles such as annuities, investments or bank products as part of your plan to help generate retirement income
- ☐ Work with your financial professional to help determine the rate per month or year to withdraw your retirement savings
- ☐ Consider consolidating retirement savings for ease of management and coordination of retirement income
- ☐ Review beneficiary designations
- ☐ Develop a will & a formal estate plan, including business succession for business owners
- ☐ Consider creating a personal trust
- ☐ Consider living on the amount of your post-retirement income prior to retirement

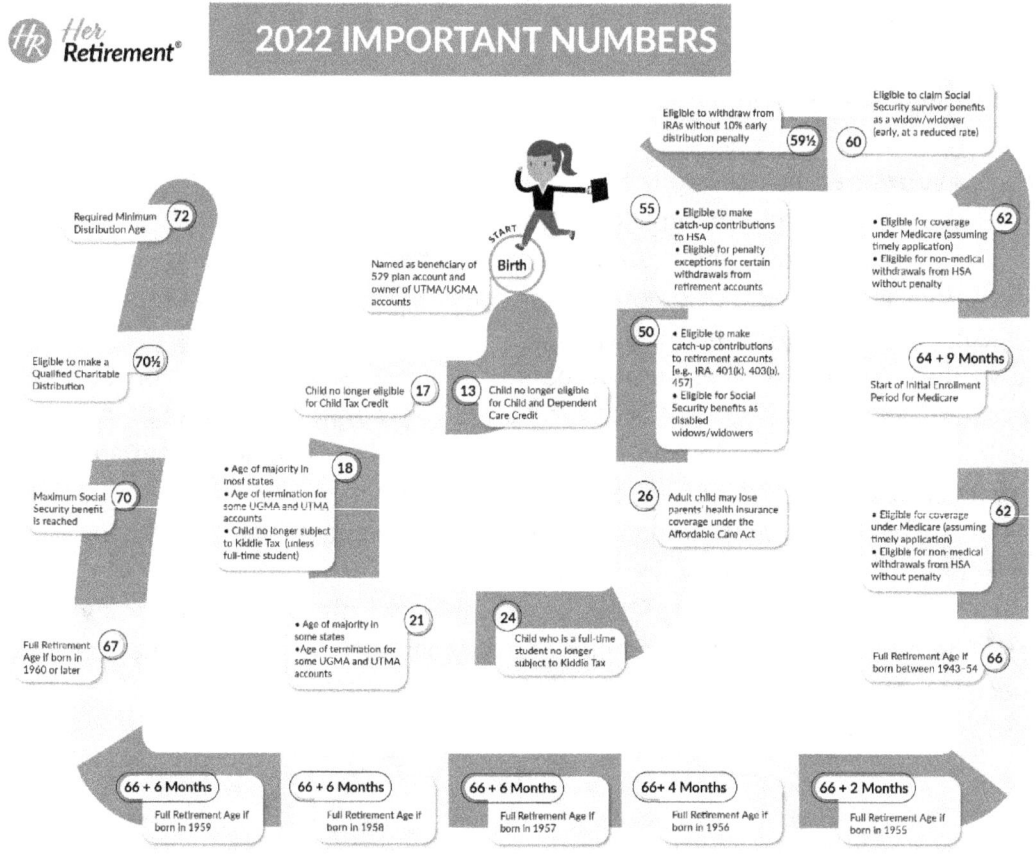

www.ingramcontent.com/pod-product-compliance
Lightning Source LLC
Chambersburg PA
CBHW060433220526

45465CB00008B/3127